A Concise Introduction
to Ventura

Also Available

A Concise Introduction to Ventura

by
J. W. Penfold

BERNARD BABANI (publishing) LTD
THE GRAMPIANS
SHEPHERDS BUSH ROAD
LONDON W6 7NF
ENGLAND

Please Note

Although every care has been taken with the production of this book to ensure that any projects, designs, modifications and/or programs etc. contained herewith, operate in a correct and safe manner and also that any components specified are normally available in Great Britain, the Publishers and Author do not accept responsibility in any way for the failure, including fault in design, of any project, design, modification or program to work correctly or to cause damage to any other equipment that it may be connected to or used in conjunction with, or in respect of any other damage or injury that may be so caused, nor do the Publishers accept responsibility in any way for the failure to obtain specified components.

Notice is also given that if equipment that is still under warranty is modified in any way or used or connected with home-built equipment then that warranty may be void.

© 1991 BERNARD BABANI (publishing) LTD

First Published — July 1991

British Library Cataloguing in Publication Data:
Penfold, J. W.
    A concise introduction to Ventura.
    1. Publishing. Use of computers
    I. Title
    070.502855369

    ISBN 0 85934 236 0

Printed and Bound in Great Britain by Cox & Wyman Limited, Reading

Preface

Desktop Publishing (DTP) is fast becoming one of the most common uses of microcomputers. Ventura Publisher is one of the most popular and powerful of the available DTP programs. This book describes Ventura as used on the IBM PC and compatible computers.

It would not be possible to describe every aspect of DTP in a book of this size, or even every feature of Ventura. This is certainly not its purpose. Rather, it is intended to give a brief introduction to the most important features and aspects, to get you started actually using the program in the shortest possible time.

This book covers the most important and useful features of the program, and also covers the vital support programs, such as those concerned with file conversion and font generation. It also covers the hardware aspects necessary to get the best use from Ventura.

DTP is one of the truly creative uses of computers. It is hoped this book will be the starting point from which you can discover both the usefulness and the pleasures of Desktop Publishing.

J. W. Penfold

Trademark Acknowledgements

MS-DOS and **Windows**
are registered trademarks of Microsoft Inc.

IBM, PC XT, PC AT, and **PC-DOS**
are registered trademarks of IBM Corporation.

GEM and **GEM ArtLine**
are registered trademarks of Digital Research Inc.

Apple, Macintosh and **LaserWriter**
are registered trademarks of Apple Corporation.

Adobe and **PostScript**
are registered trademarks of Adobe Inc.

Bitstream Fontware
is a registered trademark of Bitstream Inc.

Typografica
is a registered trademark of GST Software Ltd

Xerox Ventura Publisher
is a registered trademark of Rank Xerox plc.

ITC Avant Garde, Dingbats, ITC Bookman
and **ITC Zapf Chancery**
are registered trademarks of
International Typeface Corporation.

Contents

Chapter 1

CAPABILITY AND COMPATIBILITY

Xerox Ventura Publisher is one of the most powerful and exciting programs available for IBM PC's and compatible computers. It can be used to produce any printed matter from a letterhead to a fully illustrated book. Like most fully professional applications, it can be a little intimidating at first, as all the available facilities are somewhat too much to take in with just a quick flip through the menus. The purpose of this book is to get you past the initial panic stage, to outline the features offered and to get you started, and to give a grounding in the principles of desktop publishing (DTP), so that you can then progress to the level you need.

Making a Document
This section of this chapter gives a brief overview of the process of creating a printed document with Ventura. It also introduces some of the technical terms used. Ventura is not a program you would normally use alone, and the rest of this chapter lists the word processors and graphics programs which are suitable for use with Ventura. Hardware requirements and compatibility are covered in the second chapter. Later chapters will fill in the detail of the processes used in creating a document.

Ventura works by taking text and illustrations, and putting them together into page layouts. That is DTP in essence. However, the very wide range of text and illustrations which can be used, and the almost infinite range of page layouts which can be produced, result in a very complex and powerful program.

In fact, Ventura does include basic text entry/word processing facilities, and also basic drawing facilities, so it would be possible to produce a complete document using only Ventura. However, this is almost never done. It is much easier to produce the text on a separate word processor, which will provide better facilities for editing and modifying text, and which will certainly be faster to use. The arguments for using a separate program for producing illustrations are even stronger. Programs are available with very many more features than Ventura provides. However, the Ventura facilities are very useful for entering small pieces of text, such as headlines, and captions or short descriptions for illustrations. The graphics facilities are used mainly for decorative features such as rules and boxes.

When preparing text, there is a wide choice of word processors, as Ventura can "import" a wide variety of text file formats. It is generally not necessary to save the file in any special way, as Ventura can read the actual word processor file formats. However, if a file has been written on a word-processor which Ventura does not directly support, it may be possible to import it by saving it as a straight ASCII file. Most (but not all) word processors can produce files of this type.

Formatting text, with the exception of dividing it into paragraphs, and adding typographical features is normally done within Ventura, but some features can be included using the word processor, as Ventura will preserve them when importing the file(s). These include such things as underlining, bold text, italics, etc. Exactly what can be preserved depends on the actual word processor used. The degree of compatibility varies. These features cannot be carried across if the text has to be imported as a straight ASCII file. In this case, all formatting (with the exception of dividing into paragraphs) must be done in Ventura.

In fact, this is not strictly true, as any feature can be included when preparing text. Ventura inserts code sequences into the text file to indicate paragraph styles, font sizes, and other features. It is possible to insert these codes, which consist of ordinary characters, with the word processor when creating the file. Whether it is worth doing this depends very much on the nature of the document. Figure 1.1 is a WordPerfect 5.0 screen dump, and the first two lines include inserted Ventura code sequences.

There can be no hard and fast rules of what should be done with the word processor and what should be done in

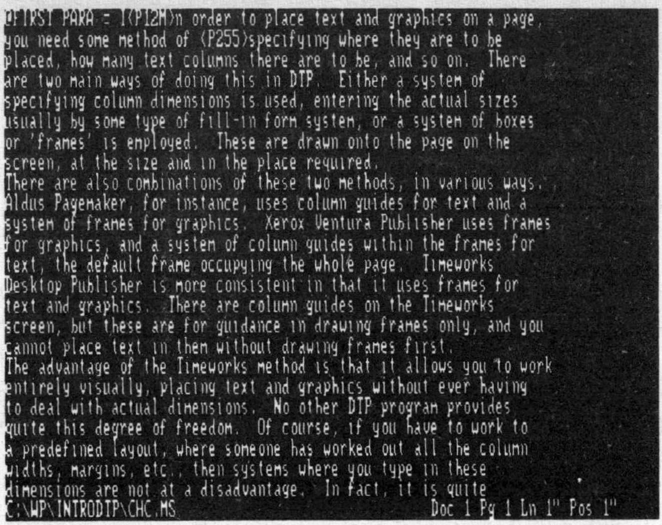
@FIRST PARA = I<P12M>n order to place text and graphics on a page, you need some method of <P255>specifying where they are to be placed, how many text columns there are to be, and so on. There are two main ways of doing this in DTP. Either a system of specifying column dimensions is used, entering the actual sizes usually by some type of fill-in form system, or a system of boxes or 'frames' is employed. These are drawn onto the page on the screen, at the size and in the place required.
There are also combinations of these two methods, in various ways. Aldus Pagemaker, for instance, uses column guides for text and a system of frames for graphics. Xerox Ventura Publisher uses frames for graphics, and a system of column guides within the frames for text, the default frame occupying the whole page. Timeworks Desktop Publisher is more consistent in that it uses frames for text and graphics. There are column guides on the Timeworks screen, but these are for guidance in drawing frames only, and you cannot place text in them without drawing frames first.
The advantage of the Timeworks method is that it allows you to work entirely visually, placing text and graphics without ever having to deal with actual dimensions. No other DTP program provides quite this degree of freedom. Of course, if you have to work to a predefined layout, where someone has worked out all the column widths, margins, etc., then systems where you type in these dimensions are not at a disadvantage. In fact, it is quite
C:\WP\INTRODTP\CHC.MS Doc 1 Pg 1 Ln 1" Pos 1"

Fig.1.1 A WordPerfect 5.0 screen with Ventura codes in a document

Ventura (though some try to make them). It is best to take an open approach and use the flexibility the program provides.

All the text files for a Ventura document do not need to be produced on the same word processor. Text from several programs and text entered with Ventura itself can be freely mixed.

With illustrations, there are again a wide variety of programs which can be used with Ventura. These fall into two types, and the difference between them is important. The first category are normally called 'paint' programs, and they produce a 'bit image', consisting of dots, normally at screen resolution. The amount of detail possible in this type of image is set when it is created, and scaling the image subsequently can only be done in a rather crude way. The second category are normally called 'draw' programs, and they produce line images. The amount of detail which can be resolved in these may increase with increasing size, and they can be scaled readily.

With graphics programs, it is important to make sure you choose a program which produces a file format which Ventura can read. There is no general purpose graphics file equivalent of the ASCII text file. If purchasing a graphics program with the express intention of using it with Ventura, it is best to go for one which produces files in the GEM formats. These are files with the .IMG extension for bit-image files, and the .GEM extension for line-image files. Suitable programs are GEM PAINT (which normally comes free with GEM DESKTOP and is not sold as a separate product) for bit images, and GEM DRAW, GEM DRAW PLUS, and GEM ARTLINE for line art.

There are programs to be found in the public domain and shareware catalogues which claim to be able to convert line images from one file format to another. Some of these may be useful. However, if you do not expect too much you will not be too disappointed. The best that can be said of some of them is that they do not *always* crash. If you need to use a conversion program you should be on the look out for certain snags.

In some cases, even if the conversion seems to have happened successfully, you may find on closer examination that parts of the drawing are missing. The most common problems are with circles and curves. Circles can be lost completely. This can also happen with curves, but they can also be incorrectly scaled (much too big, or too small and displaced), or they may be converted as a series of straight lines.

Text in the drawing can also give problems. This can occur because text consists largely of curves, but it can also be that the style used for lettering is changed, or that the lettering is rendered much too big or too small. In one case, a drawing the Author converted had all the lettering correct and in the correct relationship, but placed off to the right of the actual drawing!

It may be preferable, in any case, to add the lettering to the drawing after it has been imported into Ventura. When this is done, the Ventura fonts can be used, and this may allow a greater choice of style than the drawing program allows, higher quality, and typographical consistency with the rest of the document. The principal case where this is not possible is in the labelling of technical drawings.

Scanner graphics are a special form of bit image, produced electronically from artwork or photographs. Scanned images are normally produced in the same file formats as the output from bit-image graphics programs. The software with scanners normally provides a choice of format, and, for Ventura, it is best to choose the .IMG format. The vast majority of scanner programs can produce this file type. Failing this, the .TIF format, which is also widely supported, can be used.

The .TIF format is also used for the few scanners which can produce grey-scale information. Images of this type can be adjusted for density (lightness/darkness) and contrast by Ventura, and different types of half-tone screening can also be applied.

An important difference between the two types of graphics is that, as far as bit images are concerned, Ventura is strictly a black-and-white program. If the imported images are coloured, they will be converted to black-and-white on import. Line images, however, are supported in colour. (Note that 'line' images can include solid areas of colour, and also pattern fills.)

As text is imported, it can be placed straight on to the pages. A system of column guides within one or more 'frames', are used to define where the text is placed. There can be one or more frames on each page, and one or more columns in each frame. By default, each complete page area is bounded by a frame, and other frames can be drawn on as required. Figure 1.2 shows the Ventura screen with a two-column page layout displayed. The dotted column guides can be displayed optionally. Figure 1.3 shows an extra frame being added to this page, overlapping both columns.

A large number of predefined layouts are provided with Ventura, and you can use one of these as supplied, modify it, or design your own from scratch. A layout can be

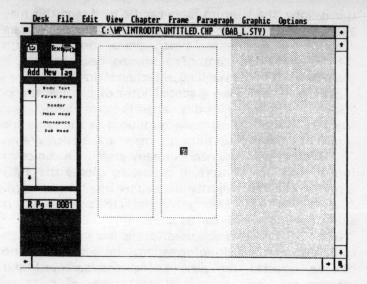

Fig.1.2   Ventura screen showing a two column page layout

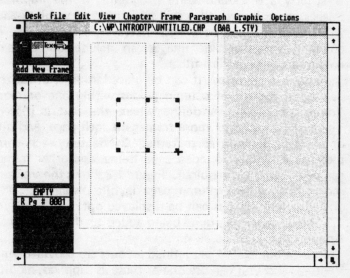

Fig.1.3   Adding a frame

saved as a 'style' for future use on other documents.

Text can be imported directly into the columns in the default frame. When this is done, the text fills the columns in the usual order, from top to bottom and from left to right. Pages will be added to the document (called a 'chapter' in Ventura) until all the text is placed. This way of working is ideal for documents like books, where one text file will cover many pages and a consistent layout is required.

Alternatively, the text can be placed in frames manually. In this case, extra pages also have to be added manually. This method is more suitable for magazine or newsletter production, where text files will not cover many pages, there may be several text files on a page, and a variety of page designs may also be used in the document.

Once text is on the page, you can go through it and make corrections, add or remove text, and add formatting features like headings. You can also select the fonts to be used. Different fonts can be used for headings, subheadings, captions, body text, etc. It is, however, a good idea not to use too many different styles and sizes.

The basic unit of text in Ventura, and indeed in most DTP programs is the paragraph, and most features are added on a paragraph by paragraph basis, though some can also be used on a character by character basis. A 'paragraph' is used in a different sense here to the usual one. A DTP paragraph is any piece of text separated from other pieces of text by delimiters, which, in Ventura, are carriage returns. Normally, one carriage return (ASCII 13 decimal) separates paragraphs, but in a pure ASCII text file, two carriage returns are required. A paragraph can be a normal paragraph, or it can be a single sentence, single word, or even a single character. It is even possible to have a 'null paragraph', with nothing at all between the delimiters.

One important point always to bear in mind is that Ventura works on the original text file. It does not make a copy to work on. This is good for minimising the amount of disk storage needed, but it does mean that the file will be changed by Ventura. Some changes are made as the file is imported. Others will be made if you do any work on the text in Ventura. If you want to keep the text file in its original form, make a copy of it *before* you import it into Ventura. An advantage of this system is that you can work on a text file which has been imported both with Ventura and with the word processor, provided you are careful not to unintentionally disturb any of the information added by Ventura.

Illustrations are not automatically placed on the page. Frames must be specifically created to place them. However, the complete area of each page is bounded by a frame. Illustrations may be placed in this. Normally, frames are 'drawn' on to the page where you want to place the graphic, and the graphic is then placed in the frame. Any text in columns under the frame is displaced. This is described as the frame 'repelling' the text, which all moves down in the document, an extra page being added automatically if there is an overflow from the last page. Figure 1.4 shows a Ventura screen with a scanned graphic and text columns.

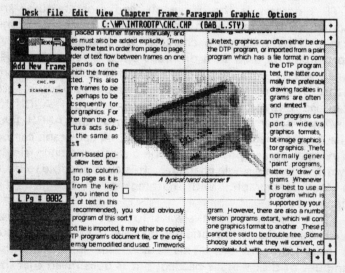

Fig.1.4 A Ventura screen with a scanned graphic and text columns

If you want to place illustrations near to particular parts of the text, it follows that the graphics must be added methodically from the first page in each chapter through to the last. When illustrations are added, text is moved, but illustrations on later pages are not. Text and illustrations can thus become separated, and trying to reunite several such instances in a chapter can become a nightmare, due to complex interactions. This does not, however, apply to *captions* to illustrations. These can be attached to their graphic, so that they will only move with it (this is shown in Figure 1.4). There are also features for automatic numbering of illustrations.

Once graphics are on the page, they can be moved and changed in size. The graphic will normally be scaled to fit the containing frame, though this behaviour can be modified. Line graphics can normally be scaled at will, though care may be necessary to ensure circles are not distorted into ellipses. Bit-image graphics can also be scaled, but this is not satisfactory if taken to extremes. Normally, scaling up is more undesirable than scaling down. Scanned line-graphic images can be scaled with the same *caveats* as bit-image graphics, but scanned photographs using dithered images should in general not be scaled at all. Remember that if an illustration is changed in size, the amount of text displaced by it will also change.

Once all the text and illustrations have been placed on the pages as required, and all headings and decorative features added, the document is ready to print, either on a dot-matrix, inkjet or laser computer printer, or, by means of a PostScript format disk file, by a professional printer using phototypesetting.

Compatibility

The word processors which can be used with Ventura, and the features which can be carried over, are described below. The word processors given here are those supported by Ventura U.K. version 2.00. Additional or different types may be available on other releases. Figure 1.5 shows the Ventura screen used to select a word processor format.

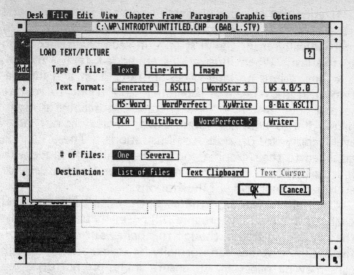

Fig.1.5 Selecting a text file format

MICROSOFT WORD (also MS Windows Write). Ventura can read and write files for Microsoft Word 3.1 directly, and other releases of Word may also work, as will some versions of Windows Write. Microsoft Word style sheets cannot be used by Ventura, however. Any graphics included in a Windows Write document may cause problems, and in any case will be lost.

The following attributes, if included in Word documents, will be converted and used by Ventura. All other attributes and features will be lost.

    Bold
    Superscript
    Subscript
    Strikethrough
    Underline
    Discretionary Hyphen
    Non-break Space

WORDPERFECT (WordPerfect Corporation). Ventura can read and write files for WordPerfect versions 4.1, 4.2, 5.0 and 5.1. The WordPerfect option (in the Load Text/ Picture menu) is used for versions 4.x, and the Word-Perfect 5.0 option for versions 5.x. Any graphics in WordPerfect 5 documents are lost.

The following WordPerfect attributes will be auto-matically converted to Ventura attributes. All other attributes and features will be lost.

Bold
Superscript
Subscript
Strikethrough
Underline
Discretionary Hyphen
Non-break Space

WORDSTAR. Ventura can read and write files for Word-Star versions 3.3, 3.4, 4.0 and 5.0. Other versions may also prove suitable.

The following WordStar attributes will be automatically converted to Ventura attributes. All other attributes and features will be lost.

Bold
Superscript
Subscript
Strikethrough
Underline
Discretionary Hyphen
Non-break Space

With WordStar 3.4, foreign characters entered into the text will only print if they are in both the IBM character set and the Ventura character set.

If preparing tabular text with WordStar, it is important to ensure that when the tab key is used, a tab character (and not multiple spaces) is inserted into the text. If this is not done, Ventura will convert the multiple spaces into single space on import, and the tabulation will be lost. To do this, ensure that the Vari-Tab feature in WordStar is *off*.

For WordStar 2000, see the section on DCA format files below.

MULTIMATE. Ventura can read and write Multimate version 3.31 files, and other versions may also prove suitable.

The following Multimate attributes will automatically be converted into Ventura attributes. All other features and attributes will be lost.

- Bold
- Superscript
- Subscript
- Strikethrough
- Underline
- Discretionary Hyphen
- Non-break Space

XEROX WRITER. Ventura can read and write Xerox Writer 2.0 files.

All Writer standard text attributes will be converted into Ventura text attributes.

XYWRITE. Ventura can read Xywrite II and III files.

All Xywrite standard text attributes are automatically converted to Ventura text attributes.

DCA. Ventura can read and write DCA version 2.0 files. Displaywrite versions III and IV can save and retrieve these files. Several other programs can convert their files into this format, but not read them.

All DCA standard text attributes are automatically converted into Ventura text attributes.

The following programs can convert or output files in DCA format. For instructions on how to do this, see the application manual or the Xerox Ventura Publisher Reference Guide, appendix D.

Lotus Manuscript
Displaywrite III
Displaywrite IV
Volkswriter 3
Office Writer
WordStar 2000
Samna Word

Other programs may also be capable of generating this format.

Graphics Programs

Ventura can import graphics from a number of graphics programs. The number of programs supported is in fact greater than the number of file formats which can be used, as there are cases where more than one graphics program uses a given file format. In fact, many graphics programs can write (if not read) several different formats, and in some cases you may have a choice of formats to export graphics to Ventura.

Scanner control programs normally 'borrow' file formats from bit-image graphics programs. These also normally offer a choice of format for saving files. Figures 1.6 and 1.7 show the Ventura screens used to select line and bit-image file formats respectively.

AUTOCAD and AUTOSKETCH. These are very popular CAD and drawing-type programs. The easiest way of transferring pictures to Ventura is to use the .SLD 'slide' format. However, although this is listed on the Ventura menu as a line-art format, it is in fact a bit-image related to the screen resolution of the computer generating it. It follows that if you have a VGA (or Super VGA with suitable driver) screen, quality may be acceptable. If you have a CGA display, it almost certainly will not.

Better quality can be obtained by using the HPGL format, but this has two drawbacks. Firstly, the file size can be massive (like megabytes rather than kilobytes) for anything other than a very simple drawing, and secondly,

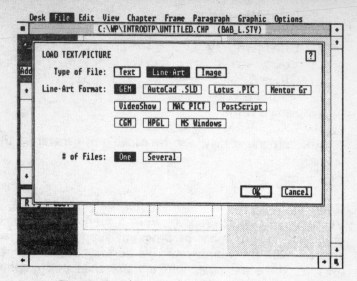

Fig.1.6 Selecting a line graphics file format

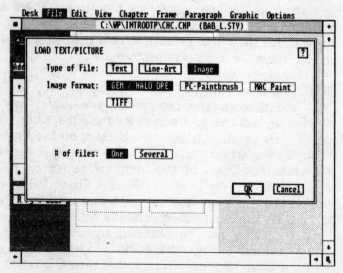

Fig.1.7 Selecting a bit-image file format

polylines and filled areas are sent to the file as a series of straight lines filling the area. Gaps between these lines can appear in the Ventura output. (Further information on HPGL files is given later.) DXF files can also be used. Ventura cannot read these directly, but a conversion utility is supplied. There are limitations on what can be converted (see below).

The new version 3 of AutoSketch can export files in Encapsulated PostScript format (see below). This will be very useful for those using PostScript printers.

CGM. This is a format used by a number of draw type programs. Ventura can read and convert these files, with the limitation that all typefaces are converted to Helvetica, and pattern fills may change. Colour is preserved.

DXF. This is a format which a number of programs (mostly CAD) use to interchange drawings. Ventura cannot read DXF files directly, but a utility is provided with Ventura (DXFTOGEM) to convert them to the GEM format, which Ventura can read. As the DXF format includes some features which are not included in the GEM format, some attributes cannot be converted. These include the following.

> Shape entity
> Text mirroring
> Tapering widths in polylines
> Underscore and overscore in text strings
> Text expansion
> Backward obliquing and arbitrary forward
>   obliquing of text
> Symbol characters in text
> Curve fitting
> 3D rendering
> Ellipses which are not X-Y aligned

ENCAPSULATED POSTSCRIPT FILES (EPS). These are a form of bit-image file, which can be generated by some scanner control programs. These files are converted, with the limitation that in some cases the image cannot be displayed on the screen (a large X is displayed in the frame), and in these cases, the files can only be printed on a PostScript printer. Use of EPS files is an advanced feature which will not be further covered.

GEM. Files with the .GEM extension are in the GEM metafile format. They are line-art files, and are read and converted by Ventura, including the version which runs under MS Windows. This is the preferred format for importing line images into Ventura. Note that GEM .IMG files created by GEM Paint also have a .GEM file associated with them. This file cannot be used for import into Ventura. Instead you must import the .IMG file as a bit-image.

GEM files are produced by GEM Draw, GEM Draw Plus, and GEM Artline. GEM Artline is particularly suitable for use with Ventura (but the newer DR Artline 2 is perhaps less so, as it needs a different release of GEM).

HPGL. Ventura can read and convert HPGL files for the HP 7470 and HP 7475 plotters. They can be generated by many graphics programs, usually by selecting to output to a plotter, and then redirecting the output to a file. HPGL files are text files which contain plotter commands which are, in principle, similar to the LOGO turtle graphics. That is, they contain commands to raise and lower the pen, and to move it, etc. As mentioned above, for anything other than simple drawings, these files can become very large indeed. Importing them can therefore be a slow business.

The following limitations apply.

> Page rotation is not supported
> Colour is not converted
> All fonts are converted to Helvetica
> Filled areas are made up of lines and may
>   show gaps
> Ends of lines may be rounded if enlarged

In general, the use of HPGL files is only to be recommended if there is no alternative.

GEM .IMG Files. Files with the .IMG extension are in the GEM bit-image format. These are produced by GEM Paint, the GEM Snapshot screen capture utility, and some other graphics programs. GEM Scan and many other scanner control programs can also produce .IMG files. This is the preferred format for importing bit images into Ventura. The only limitation is that colours are not converted, as Ventura is strictly a black-and-white program where bit images are concerned, and that special attention may be necessary to print dithered scanner images at optimum quality.

LOTUS 1-2-3. Lotus 1-2-3 .PIC files are read and converted.

MACINTOSH PAINT. Files from Macintosh Paint can be transferred to Ventura using a network or a communications program. Pictures always transfer as a full 8 x 10 inch page, so a small image will need to be enlarged to fill the frame.

MACINTOSH PICT. These files are converted, using a network or comms program to transfer them. However, bit images within PICT files do not convert, and text fonts are converted to Times Roman (usually) or Helvetica (occasionally).

PC PAINTBRUSH .PCX. This is the native format used by PC Paintbrush, and is also used by, or available as an option in, several other graphics programs. It is a bit-image format, and is also used by many scanners. These files are converted by Ventura, but colour is not converted, the images becoming black-and-white.

TAGGED IMAGE FILE FORMAT (TIFF or .TIF). This format is mostly generated by scanner control software. It can be either a bit-image format, or a grey-scale format.

This is the only format in which Ventura can import scanner images with true grey-scale data. When imported in this form, it is possible to alter the lightness/darkness and contrast of the image within Ventura, as well as certain other features. However, very few scanners can generate grey-scale data. Most produce a 'dithered' image direct. The HP ScanJet is the best-known scanner with grey-scale capability.

Chapter 2

HARDWARE REQUIREMENTS

The basic system requirements for Ventura Publisher are:

640K of main RAM memory
MS-DOS 3.1 or higher, or compatible
    operating system
A hard disk with a minimum of about 5 megabytes
    free before installation
A suitable mouse or other pointing device
    (e.g. graphics tablet)
A graphics display card and monitor.

This chapter gives details of some of these.

CPU and Memory
Ventura Publisher can run on any of the IBM PC computers or compatibles, which means it can use any CPU from the 8088 upwards. However, with the 8088, some operations are likely to be rather slow. Graphics scaling is one, and any screen redraws where graphics are involved are also likely to be protracted.

If choosing a computer with the intention of running Ventura on it, it would be best to consider one based on the 80386 or 80386SX (these are now sometimes called the 386DX and 386SX respectively). These will give faster operation, and have features which can make memory management easier.

Ventura runs under MS-DOS or a compatible operating system, such as PC-DOS and DR-DOS. These operating systems can directly address 1 megabyte (1024K) of memory, of which 384K is used up by system ROMs, screen memory, disk controllers and similar (and much may be unused), and up to 640K is RAM. If more RAM than this is fitted in a machine, it cannot (with one exception, mentioned later) be directly used by DOS or Ventura. There are, however, ways of using additional memory.

Ventura requires a full 640K of DOS base memory to be fitted. Even with this amount of memory, problems may be experienced. It is important to make sure that no unnecessary memory-resident programs are running. These can include DOS device drivers, pop-up programs, and such things as on-screen clocks and screen-dump utilities.

Device drivers are loaded automatically on start-up, and are included in the file CONFIG.SYS. This is similar to a batch file, and is run automatically by DOS immediately after it has loaded. Device drivers are listed in this file, and have the .SYS file extension. If you have memory problems, the drivers you may be able to remove include ANSI.SYS and RAMDRIVE.SYS.

ANSI.SYS (which may be called something like V7ANSI.SYS, depending on what graphics card you have) is concerned only with the text screen. It is not used by Ventura, and indeed is not much used by text-based programs, so you may be able to gain a few K by removing this.

RAMDRIVE.SYS creates a virtual disk drive in RAM. If you have a computer based on an 8088, like the original IBM PC, or the 8086, like several Amstrad and Olivetti models, the virtual disk, as well as the device driver, will be using up main memory. You will almost certainly have to remove this driver to run Ventura. On AT-type computers, using the 80286, 80386 or 80486, the actual memory used for the virtual disk may be in extended memory, that is, memory above the first megabyte. In this case, the RAMDRIVE.SYS line will be something like

device=C:\DOS\ramdrive.sys 384 /e

The " /e " puts the virtual disk in extended memory. A small amount of base memory will also be used, but this may be insignificant. If you have extra memory fitted, and this cannot be used as EMS memory (see later) it is a good idea to have a RAM disk in extended memory, as Ventura can use this for overflow and temporary files.

To enable this, you must add " /0=d: " to the line of the file VP.BAT (which is created automatically when you install Ventura) which begins with "DRVRMRGR". The " d: " represents the drive letter for your virtual disk. For example, here is the batch file from the Author's machine, where the virtual disk is drive E:.

```
C:
CD \VENTURA
INT16
DRVRMRGR VP %1 /S=SD_VGA_5.VGA/M=03/0=E:
C:
CD \VENTURA
INT16 X
CD\
```

Other parts of this line, and your batch file, may be different, depending on what screen and mouse you are using.

One device driver you should not remove, if you have it, is HIMEM.SYS. This driver, which is provided with some versions of MS-DOS, and with Microsoft Windows, is an expanded memory manager, and with it, Ventura can exploit a 64K block of extended memory. This block is the first above the 1 megabyte limit, and, due to a quirk in the 8088 processor family, can be addressed directly. This block of memory is only available with 80286 or higher CPUs, and only if more than 640K of RAM is fitted. Even if these conditions are met, not all machines make this block available.

Having this block available does make a big difference to the use and performance of Ventura. It was only by exploiting this block that the screen dumps in this book could be produced.

Pop-up programs and resident utilities, often collectively referred to as Terminate and Stay Resident (TSR) programs, are often loaded in the file AUTOEXEC.BAT. Like CONFIG.SYS, this file is run automatically, in fact immediately after CONFIG.SYS. In order to run Ventura successfully, you should remove all TSRs from this file. It is especially important to remove any big pop-up programs, like Borland's SideKick, or pop-up text editors. There is no chance of Ventura loading with these present.

Expanded and Extended Memory
There are two ways in which extra memory may be added to an MS-DOS system. It can either be added to the memory map above the 1 megabyte DOS limit, or it can be addressed indirectly, using a 'window' in the first megabyte area. The first of these methods is called extended memory, because it extends the memory map, sometimes abbreviated to XMS. The second is called expanded memory, and is also commonly called LIM memory or EMS.

Extra memory on the computer motherboard is usually extended memory. Memory added on a card is normally expanded memory.

The only form of extended memory Ventura can use is the first 64K block mentioned previously, if available. Any other expanded memory is inaccessible as such to Ventura However, drivers are available which enable expanded memory to be addressed as extended memory, and if one of these is used the extra memory can be employed. Drivers of this type have a name something like EMM. SYS, and are included in the CONFIG.SYS file. Many of these can only be used with 80386 (including SX) or 80486 CPUs.

If expanded memory conforming to the LIM/EMS specification is fitted, Ventura can use this, without any special requirements. When extra memory is available, much larger documents can be handled. Expanded memory can be fitted to just about any PC, including those based on the 8088 CPU. The standard version of Ventura will put up to 90K of system files in expanded memory if available. If you have the professional extension, up to 32 megabytes of EMS memory can be utilised.

The Screen
Venture uses a runtime version of GEM, and this provides the screen handling. You can therefore use any screen which is supported by GEM. Ventura is a graphically-based

program, and requires a graphics screen. It cannot be used with a text-only display.

GEM drivers are available for all standard IBM PC displays, and for many non-standard ones. A wide selection is provided with Ventura. If you have a display which is not on the list, it is worth checking with Digital Research (not Xerox) to see if a suitable driver is available, as new types are added from time to time. Alternatively, your display may be usable with one of the standard drivers, perhaps at less than its maximum resolution.

The drivers include some of the latest 'Super VGA' modes, offering 800 x 600 resolution. Ventura can also drive colour displays. However, it may not be in your best interests to select the highest display specification available to you. For example, the Author has a display card capable of 800 x 600, but when used, this reduces the actual display area on the monitor screen (due to the monitor rather than the card). It is therefore much more comfortable to use 640 x 480 resolution. Also, if the program is not used for colour work, it is better to install a 2-colour (black and white) driver rather than a 16-colour one. This saves some memory space and will give faster screen handling.

Ventura can be used with special 'portrait' format screens which allow a full A4 page to be displayed, and also with very large displays which can show two facing pages. There are also special displays which allow a fast 'hardware pan' around the page on-screen. These displays require special drivers, and often special driver cards to be fitted in the computer. Such displays are often sold as complete packages.

The Printer
In theory, if you intend using Ventura to have documents printed professionally from PostScript files, you do not need a printer at all. However, most people will want to be able to print their own documents.

It is often implied that only a laser printer is good enough for DTP, but this is not really true. Though a resolution of 300 dots per inch (DPI) is desirable, results at lower resolutions are acceptable for some purposes. Ventura can drive printers down to 9-pin dot matrix types, at 120 x 144 DPI, though the quality produced by these is, perhaps, not quite good enough for anything other than proofing.

If a PostScript-compatible laser printer is used, it has the advantage that documents can be printed to disk or collected by a Fast Access Retrieval Terminal (the only thing in computing not to have an acronym) and printed professionally without requiring any modifications. However, PostScript does have some limitations, particularly in how graphics and text can be overlaid, and if documents are never to be printed professionally, the use of a non-PostScript printer may be preferred.

As with displays, printers are handled through GEM. A selection of drivers is provided, and other types may be available from Digital Research. The Author has printed to a Hewlett-Packard PaintJet printer using a driver actually supplied with GEM ArtLine. GEM 3.1 drivers are compatible with the version of GEM supplied with Ventura. GEM 3.0 drivers are not. The driver must be copied into the VENTURA subdirectory.

You must also have printer fonts compatible with the printer you wish to use. With PostScript printers, the fonts are included in the printer, though others can be stored on disk in the computer and downloaded before printing. Other types of printer may also use built-in or downloadable fonts. These include printers which use Hewlett-Packard's Page Compilation Language (PCL).

Other printer types use fonts which are stored in the computer, and finished documents are sent to the printer as a graphics dump. Ventura comes with sets of fonts for all the supported printers, and these may also be suitable for use with other types. For example, the HP Paintjet printer can use the same fonts as 24-pin dot-matrix printers (180 x 180 DPI). Other fonts can be added with a font-generation program, of which several are available. This is described in a separate chapter.

The main problem if you use a printer not supported directly by Xerox is with the font width files. These files, which have an extension of .WID, are used to tell Ventura which fonts are available for a given printer, and also the widths of each character in each font. Width tables 'belong' to a particular printer, and if you try to use one with the 'wrong' printer, Ventura will only accept it as a draft quality table, and not try to use all the available fonts, even if the two printers require the same fonts.

If you have a width table for a compatible printer, it is possible to modify it if you have a direct file editor (sometimes called 'sector editors'). Suitable editors are often found in utility suites such as PC Tools. You should not attempt to do this with a text editor or word processor. Also, it is essential that the two printers are genuinely compatible as regards font files. The example here is for the Epson LQ series and HP PaintJet, which both use 180 DPI fonts.

Firstly, after copying the printer driver into the Ventura subdirectory, you must determine the name by which GEM identifies the printer. You can do this by looking at the SET PRINTER INFO dialogue box, from the OPTIONS menu (see Figure 2.1). This lists all available printers. Make a note of the exact name displayed for the printer you are adding.

Next, quit Ventura, and make a copy of the width table for the compatible printer under a new name. If you now examine this file with the file editor, you will find that the name of the compatible printer is at the very beginning (see Figure 2.2). You simply have to change this name to the one of the printer you are adding (see Figure 2.3). If you now re-start Ventura, and select this width file from the Add/Remove Fonts dialogue box (OPTIONS menu), Ventura should now accept the fonts for Ultimate quality (see Figure 2.4).

Mice

Although in theory it is possible to use Ventura from the keyboard without a mouse, it is doubtful if anyone could do it for more than an hour or so and remain sane. Most popular mice can be used with Ventura, and it is also

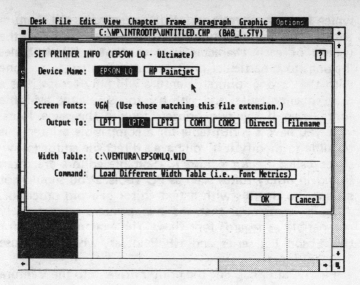

Fig.2.1 Finding a printer name

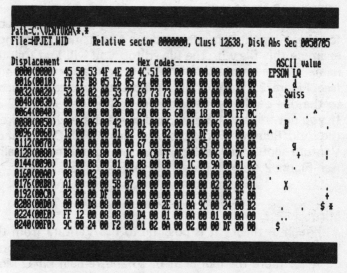

Fig.2.2 The start of a printer width file

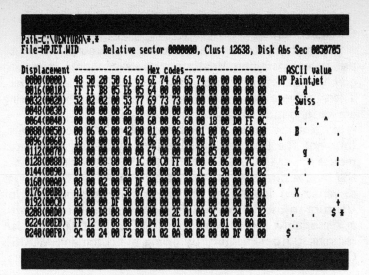

Fig.2.3 The width file after modification

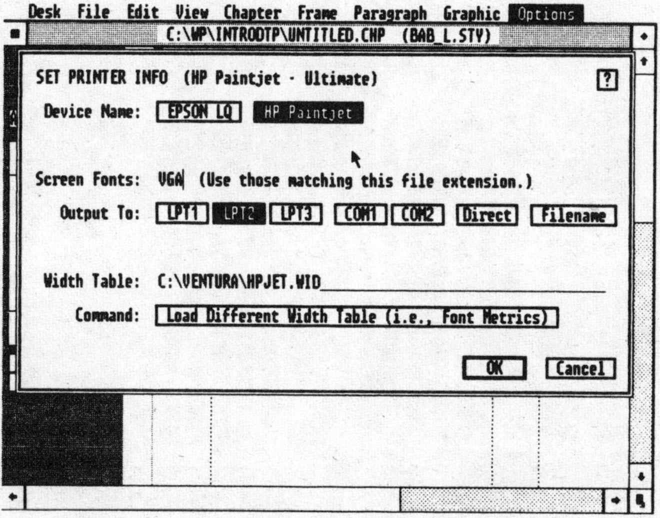

Fig.2.4 The modified width file loaded

possible to use some graphics tablets, such as the SummaGraphics.

Normally, you select the mouse type you are going to use when installing Ventura. However, some mice and graphics tablets may need drivers which are not included. These drivers are normally supplied with the pointing device, and may need separate installation.

With some mice, such as the Microsoft Serial Mouse (but not the Bus version), Ventura by-passes the normal mouse driver (MOUSE.COM or MOUSE.SYS) and addresses the mouse directly. In these cases, it is better if the mouse driver is not loaded, as this leaves more memory free for Ventura to use. If you are using the Microsoft mouse with a reasonably recent version of MOUSE.COM, you can remove it from memory by giving the command MOUSE OFF from the DOS prompt, before starting Ventura.

Chapter 3

LAYOUT AND PARAGRAPH STYLES

In order to place text and graphics on a page, you need some method of specifying where they are to be placed, how many text columns there are to be, and so on. There are two mains ways of doing this in DTP. Either a system of specifying column dimensions is used, entering the actual sizes usually by some type of fill-in form system, or a system of boxes or 'frames' is employed. These are drawn onto the page on the screen, at the size and in the place required.

There are also combinations of these two methods. Ventura uses a system of frames, with column guides within them for text. Whole frames are used for graphics. It is not possible to have both text and graphics in the same frame, but it is possible to overlap frames.

There is a main frame on each page, which occupies the full area of the page. In fact, it is called the 'page frame'. It does not have to be the full size of the paper you are using, however. In this way you can produce a document of any size, though Ventura will only print on certain standard sheet sizes. This frame has special significance, as the column guides created within it will be repeated on every page in the document. This basic layout of columns (together with other things) can be saved as a style sheet. With documents having left and right pages, a different layout can be specified for each side.

With Ventura, it is a good idea to select or design the style of a document before starting to import text and graphics. Though modifications can be made after you have begun putting the document together, a major re-design can be awkward and involve a lot of extra work. You must have a style loaded to use Ventura, and in fact, when it starts up, Ventura will always load the style you were using in the previous session.

Ventura comes with a wide selection of predefined styles. These are listed and described in the manual

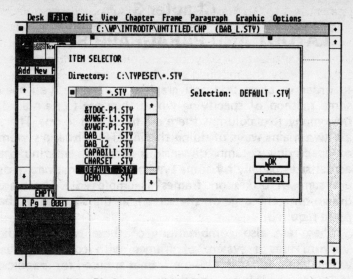

Fig.3.1 Loading DEFAULT.STY

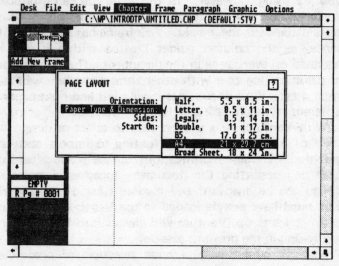

Fig.3.2 Selecting paper size

(appendix L). To start with, you will probably be able to find something among these that will suit your purpose. However, eventually you will want to have more control over the appearance of your documents. You can then either modify the supplied styles, or create your own from scratch.

Designing a Style

To design a new style, you can either start with an existing style which is similar to what you want, or you can start with the blank style file DEFAULT.STY. In either case, you can save your style under a new name when complete, so you need not lose the original style. (To avoid any possibility of overwriting the blank DEFAULT.STY, you can set the file to read-only using the DOS ATTRIB utility.) You load a new style from the FILE menu. See Figure 3.1.

The first thing to set is the size of paper you will be using. Note that the size of your document does not have to be the same as the paper size. You can make it any smaller size. You can choose one of seven standard paper sizes. Figure 3.2 shows the page layout dialogue box, selected from the CHAPTER menu. In this dialogue box you also select either portrait or landscape orientation. This determines whether the long side of the paper is vertical (portrait) or horizontal (landscape).

Other options are Sides, which lets you select whether to print on one or both sides of the paper (i.e. whether your document will have left and right hand pages), and whether you want the first page to be left-hand or right-hand. Figure 3.3 shows all these options.

The size of your document is set by the size of the page frame. This is done with the Sizing and Scaling dialogue box, from the FRAME menu. You simply enter the width and height required as the Frame Width and Frame Height. The default values for these will be the same as the paper size. If you set a frame size smaller than the paper size, it is a good idea to also set Upper Left X and Upper Left Y. These will move the page frame in towards the centre of the paper by the amounts specified. This leaves room for

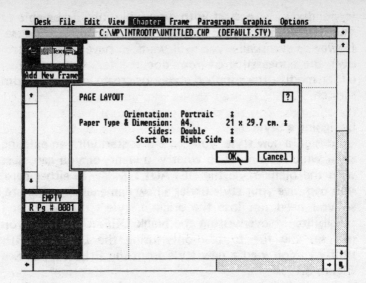

Fig.3.3 Page layout options

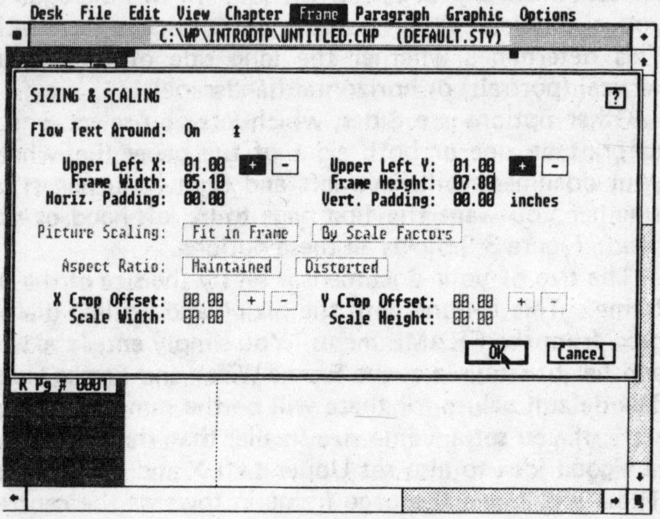

Fig.3.4 Setting the page frame

cropping marks to be included when the document is printed. Figure 3.4 shows this dialogue box. (The values entered in the figures are to produce a layout approximating to that used for this book.)

The Margins and Columns dialogue, also from the FRAME menu, is used to set the number and spacing of the columns. You can choose to have from 1 to 8 columns. In this dialogue box, you can set the widths of the columns, which is the actual width which will be occupied by print, and the gutter width, which is the white space between the printed areas. Separate widths can be set for each column, and each individual gutter between pairs of columns.

You also set the margins in this dialogue box. These are the unused areas at top and bottom of the page, and also to the left of the leftmost column, and to the right of the rightmost column. However, note that the side margin, column, and gutter widths interact. These cannot (obviously) add up to more than the width of the frame, so if you alter the margin settings, you may find one or more of the column or gutter settings are changed. The calculated and actual frame widths are displayed below the margin settings. See Figure 3.5.

Note that if you print headers and/or footers on your pages, these are printed within the top and bottom margins respectively. The settings you make in this dialogue are strictly for the required text printing areas.

If your document has left and right pages, you can set completely different layouts for the two sides. If you want a mirror-image layout, you can do this quickly by clicking on the Copy To Facing Page button.

This completes the basic page layout. There are various other settings which can be made, such as Widows and Orphans, but the defaults are well chosen and it is rarely necessary to alter them. Auto-Numbering and Footnote settings can also be made, but these features are beyond the scope of this introductory book. It can be a good idea to save the style under a new name at this point, prior to defining the paragraph styles.

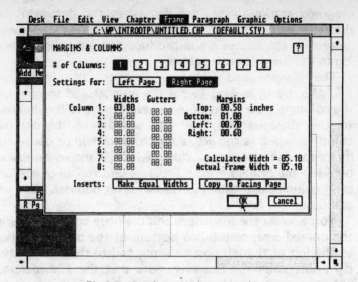

Fig.3.5 Setting margins and columns

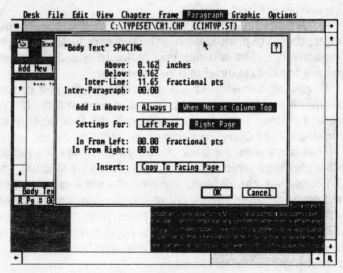

Fig.3.6 Spacing dialogue box

Paragraph Styles

The ability to predefine paragraph styles is an important tool in maintaining a consistent style throughout a document. 'Paragraph' in this context includes such things as headings and subheadings.

In order to define paragraph styles, you need to have a text file loaded. You must then select paragraph mode from the mode selector, and highlight a paragraph by clicking with the text cursor anywhere in the paragraph.

When defining a paragraph, you can set the font (style and size) to be used for that paragraph. These are selected from the Fonts option on the PARAGRAPH menu. It is possible to set any style (bold, italic, underlined) as the default for a paragraph, though of course this can be overridden on a character-by-character basis. For body text, you would, of course, normally choose normal. Other settings can be useful for headings.

The Body Text paragraph style is the first to set. You must always have a paragraph style of this name. It is used by default for all text added to the document, whether from the keyboard or as imported files, unless paragraphs in a file have been pre-tagged with another style, and that style is defined.

In Ventura, you can set both spacing above and spacing below each paragraph. It is important to understand how these work. When you have one paragraph above another, either the space below the top paragraph or the space above the lower paragraph will be left as a horizontal margin between them. The larger of the two is used. They are *not* added together. For body text it makes sense to make these two settings identical, and also to set the Add in Above setting to 'When Not at Column Top'. Figure 3.6 shows the SPACING dialogue box.

To divide body text *visually* into paragraphs, you can either add extra space between paragraphs, indent the first line of each, or both. The first method is appropriate to layouts where you are using a lot of white space. The second helps to fit the maximum of text into a given space. The third can look overdone unless the extra space is kept small.

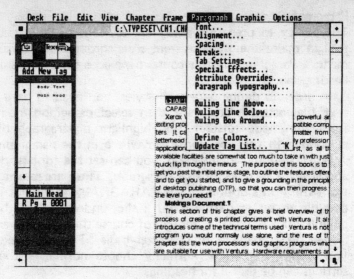

Fig.3.7   The PARAGRAPH menu

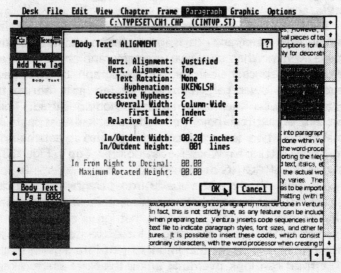

Fig.3.8   The alignment dialogue box

36

By default, Ventura uses the method of allowing extra space, as seen in Figure 3.6. To use the alternative method, the space above and space below settings should both be set to zero. The space between paragraphs will then be the same as the inter line space. The indent is set on the Alignment dialogue box.

On the Spacing dialogue, you also set 'In From Left' and 'In From Right'. These allow you to make the width of the paragraph less than the width of the column (or frame in some circumstances). This is often done for paragraphs which are quotations. It is also necessary to inset the paragraph from the left if you want to use a 'hanging indent' or 'outdent'.

The ALIGNMENT dialogue box is selected from the PARAGRAPH menu (see Figures 3.7 and 3.8). Horizontal alignment lets you choose left, centre, right, justified or decimal alignment. Left alignment will give a ragged right margin. Some people prefer this for body text, and it is also useful for sub-headings. Centred alignment is useful for headings or for special effects. If used for substantial text, it gives equal left and right indents to each line. Right alignment gives an even right margin, with a ragged left margin, and is perhaps the least used. Justified is perhaps the most common for body text. It causes the text to be forced to fill the overall width, by adding extra space between characters as necessary.

Decimal alignment is used to align columns of figures on the decimal point. If you select this, you can also set In From Right To Decimal, which, fairly obviously, sets how far in the decimal point will be from the right margin.

Vertical alignment controls how the paragraph will be placed in the column if it is not completely filled. Top alignment is the most useful setting here, especially for body text. Alternatives are middle and bottom alignment. If the column is completely filled, this setting has no effect.

Overall Width sets whether the column guide width or the frame width will be used. Using full frame width lets you place headings across the whole width of a page when using multiple columns, and would most commonly be

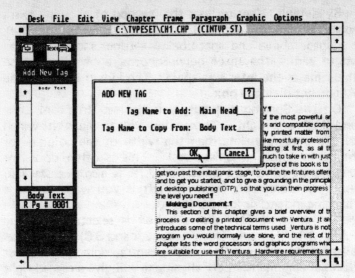

Fig.3.9   Entering a new tag name

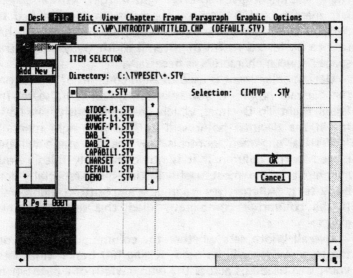

Fig.3.10   Saving a style

used in conjunction with centred alignment.

If you want to indent the first line of each paragraph, set the First Line setting to Indent, and set the In/Outdent width to the amount of indentation required. Outdents or hanging indents are set similarly. Note that the width setting is an actual dimension, not a number of characters. You should not use a tab setting to indent first lines.

All the body text will take on the new characteristics as soon as you click on the OK box.

Adding New Tags

A paragraph style in Ventura is called a tag, as new paragraphs can be tagged with it. To add a new tag, you must be in paragraph mode, and must highlight a paragraph which you want to change to the new style. If you have already created a tag similar to the one you want to add, you can tag the paragraph with this style first. This will minimise the changes involved.

You must first give the new tag a name. To do this, click on the Add New Tag box under the mode selector. This will bring up a dialogue box, and you can enter the name for your tag. See Figure 3.9. The steps are then the same as described above for setting the Body Text style, except that some or all of the settings will be different.

With paragraph styles, as with fonts, it is generally a mistake to use too many different ones within one document. The result of doing so is to produce a document which is either messy, or which gives a rather lightweight, sensationalistic, impression. You may need up to three or four heading styles, a body text style, and you may also need a special style for quotations, usually like body text but more indented, and perhaps a special style for introductory paragraphs, or a bullet style as described previously. Think very carefully about using more than this.

Saving Styles

Having developed a style for a document, you may well want to use that style for other, related, documents. It would be a nuisance if you had to do all the work of designing page layouts and specifying paragraph styles again, so most DTP programs have some means of allowing the overall design, without text or illustrations, to be saved, as a *style sheet*. See Figure 3.10.

In Ventura, the things which are saved as the style are the paper size, the main frame size together with the column guide positions and dimensions, and the paragraph styles. Settings for auto-numbering, footnotes, widow and orphan settings, and the printer width table are also saved. Settings for other frames are saved in individual chapter files, as are header and footer settings.

You save the style by selecting 'Save as New Style' from the FILES menu. You must enter a new name for your style. The current chapter will thereafter be associated with this style.

If you make changes to a style sheet and do not save it under a new name, the changes can be saved as modifications to the style. Note that if you do this, these changes will also affect any other chapters which use the same style, and on which you work subsequently.

Chapter 4

TEXT

It is normally convenient to prepare text using a word processor program, rather than entering it directly, making sure that the word processor you choose has a file format in common with Ventura. It is also wise to check how many of the features inserted in the text during word processing are recognised and preserved. These features include such things as emboldening, italicising and underlining.

If you have difficulties with compatibility, it is worth remembering that Ventura can import straight ASCII files, and that most word processors can save files in this format. However, when this is done, features such as underlining and emboldening can only be included by inserting special character sequences into the text. This process is described later.

A text file imported from a word processor can be made to flow from frame to frame, or column to column. Subsequent editing is also possible. As you insert text, all the text below it moves down, flowing to the next frame or column where necessary. The only point you have to check is whether any of the text has flowed out of the last frame in the document.

When a text file is imported into Ventura with the default frame active, it is automatically placed in the frame, filling up the columns in top-to-bottom and left-to-right order. The file is placed, starting with the current page, and new pages are added to the document as necessary, without any action being necessary on the user's part. If no frame is active, the text must be placed into frames manually, using the mouse to select them. In this case, new pages must be added manually as required, until all the text in the file has been placed. If a frame other than the default is active, the text will be placed first into this frame, but any left over will not be placed automatically into any other frame, even if there are identical frames on every page. The rest of the text must be placed manually.

When a text file is imported into Ventura, it is modified by the program. Formatting codes are inserted directly into it. This method avoids the generation of very large files, and blocking up disk space with duplicated material, and it also means that the text file can be loaded back into the word processor for further editing (taking care not to corrupt the formatting characters which the DTP program inserts). However, you do have to be careful not to delete the text file while you are still working on the document.

If you want to keep an unmodified copy of the document for other purposes, you must make a copy file, and use that for importing into Ventura. It is important to remember this, as converting back from the Ventura codes to the original word-processor format can only be done manually, and it is a long and irksome task. The Author's preferred way of doing this is to copy the text file from the word processor subdirectory to the TYPESET directory which is created when Ventura is installed.

Importing a Text File
To import a text file, you select Load Text/Picture from the FILE menu. You will be presented with a series of dialogue boxes. In the first, you must select the type of file you want to import, text or picture, and the program you want to import from. You can only import files of one format in one operation; however, you can choose to import several files in one go.

If you want the text file to be directly placed onto pages, it is best to make the page frame active before starting importing. You do this simply by entering frame mode and clicking anywhere within the page frame that is not also within another frame. This will ensure that all the text is placed, adding as many pages as necessary.

It is possible to place all the text in one operation if it has been imported with the page frame inactive. This is done by making the page frame active, as above, then clicking on the name of the text file in the file list. However, some actions seem to inhibit this, such as if you have drawn additional frames, and you may find you have to add pages manually to place the complete file.

It will be necessary to place the text and add new pages manually if you want to place the file in frames other than the page frame. Typically, you might want to do this if you are creating a free-form document like a newsletter or leaflet, rather than a book-style document (to which Ventura is more suited). In this case, the text must be placed frame-by-frame, but if you have more than one column in the frames, they will be filled automatically in left-to-right order.

You must place the text by making each frame to take it active in turn, then clicking on the name of the file in the file list. New pages must be added as required, by choosing the Insert/Remove Page option in the PAGE menu, and selecting Insert New Page After Current Page. When a file is placed over several frames in this way, if subsequent editing adds or removes text, flow from frame to frame will occur, keeping the text in order. However, any overflow from the last frame will be unplaced. You need to check for this, and to add an additional frame if necessary. Extensive deletion could also leave you with an empty frame.

Paragraph Tagging

When a text file is imported, unless paragraph tags have been incorporated into it, as described below, all paragraphs will initially be in Body Text style. Assuming that all required paragraph styles have been included in the style sheet, the first job to do is to go through the text and to tag all appropriate paragraphs with the required styles.

To tag paragraphs, you must be in Paragraph mode, selected from the mode selector. To tag a paragraph, first highlight it by clicking with the mouse cursor anywhere within that paragraph. You then simply click on the name of the tag required in the Assignment List (see Figure 4.1). The paragraph will take on the new style immediately.

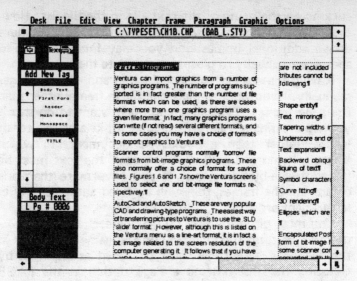

Fig.4.1 Selecting a paragraph tag

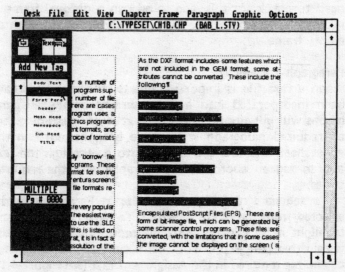

Fig.4.2 Selecting multiple paragraphs

44

It is possible to select multiple paragraphs for tagging. This is often useful for tabular data, where each paragraph may consist of a single line. To do this, hold down the shift key whilst clicking on each paragraph. Clicking again on a paragraph will de-select it. 'Multiple' will be displayed in the Current Selection indicator (see Figure 4.2). When the tag is selected, it will be applied to all paragraphs highlighted. Note that any highlighted paragraph which is moved off the screen (e.g., by scrolling) will be de-selected.

To move from page to page when moving through the text you can either select Go To Page from the CHAPTER menu, or use the page up (PgUp) and page down (PgDn) keys. Using the keys is considerably faster for moving to the next or previous page. The Go To Page dialogue is convenient to move to a specific page number or to the first or last page (see Figure 4.3).

When using the reduced view (VIEW menu) to view full pages on the screen, small text sizes may be 'greeked', which means they will appear as grey areas rather than as individual characters (see Figure 4.4). Despite this, paragraphs can still be highlighted and tagged, though if you cannot read the text there is obviously a danger of assigning an inappropriate tag. It is better to use the Normal or, if necessary, the Enlarged view, so that all text is readable, and to move around the page with the scroll bars.

Note that most paragraph styles will take up more space than the Body Text style, so as you tag the file, it will take up more space. If the file was loaded into the page frame, so that pages were added automatically to take it, extra pages will be added as necessary to take the overflow. If you placed the text manually, you will have to check for any overflow, and add frames or pages as necessary.

As you tag paragraphs, it may be that in some cases the results are not entirely satisfactory. In such cases, you may want to adjust the paragraph style. It is perfectly in order to do this, but remember that if you change the style sheet, the changes will affect any other document using this style. This helps to ensure a consistent style is maintained throughout a multi-chapter document, but a

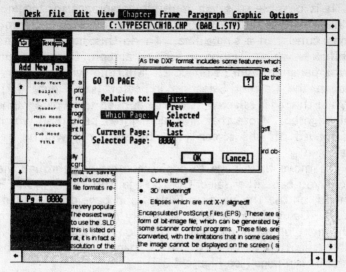

Fig.4.3   The Go To Page dialogue box

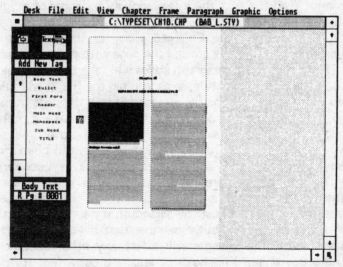

Fig.4.4   Greeked text in reduced view

change which helps in one place could hinder in another. It may be better to make the change as a new paragraph style, rather than as a modification to an existing one. The new style would become available to other documents using the style sheet, but would not cause any changes in them.

Modifying Text Attributes
As well as being able to set the font (typeface and size) and style (normal, bold, italic, etc.) for entire paragraphs as part of the paragraph style, it is also possible to alter these on a character-by-character basis. You must be in text mode, set from the mode selector, to do this.

The text to be altered, which can be anything from a single character upwards, must first be highlighted. To do this, move the cursor to just before the first character to be altered, and then drag it to just after the last character to be altered. Alternatively, move the cursor to just before the first character, hold down the shift key, and move the cursor to just after the last character.

The font can be altered by clicking on Set Font (see Figure 4.5). This brings up the font selection dialogue box. You then simply select the font to which you want to change the text. The change will take effect as soon as you click on OK. Note that the text is not automatically de-selected by this action.

Bold and italic attributes could be set by selecting a font of this type if available. If not, they can be selected from the list of styles, as can underlining, etc. If a font with the required attributes is not available, Ventura will generate a bold or italic version of the normal (roman) font, both for the screen display and the printed document.

Entering Text Directly
Ventura includes facilities for entering text directly. Text entered in this way is stored as a text file separate from the chapter file, and in some circumstances can be subsequently edited with a word processor or text editor. This opens up the possibilities of using a spelling checker on it.

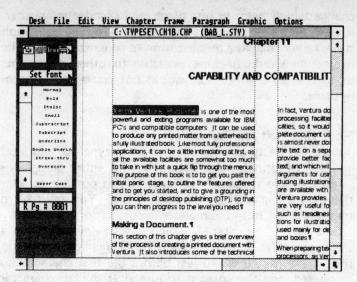

Fig.4.5   Selecting 'Set Font'

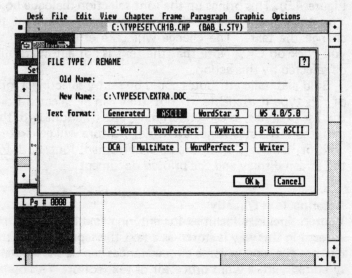

Fig.4.6   Naming a file for directly entered text

If text is entered into a document which does not have any other text in it (i.e. no files have been imported), it is immediately accepted. When the chapter is saved, the text file will be saved with a name that has the same base name as that which you give the chapter, but a different extension.

If you have already placed a text file (or files) in the document, this automatic naming cannot be used. If you try to add text to the document (other than inserting or adding it to one of the files, i.e., on a blank page) you will be asked to enter the name of a file to take the text. This must be a new filename. You can choose to save this file in the format of any of the word processors supported by Ventura (see Figure 4.6). This allows the possibility of using that word processor for subsequent editing or spelling checking. Once you have given this file name, you can begin entering text.

A file created like this will appear in the file list, and can be treated like any other text file. It can thus be made to flow between frames and pages, something which other DTP programs are not able to do with directly entered text.

Editing Text

Within Ventura, text can be edited much as in a word processor. Text can be typed in at the cursor position, or deleted. Block delete and move (cut/copy/paste) operations are also supported. However, there is no search and replace provision.

To perform any of these operations, you must be in text mode, selected from the mode selector.

To add text, you simply move the cursor to the position where you want to add the text, and start typing. The backspace and delete keys can be used to correct mistakes in the usual way. Text can be added in insert mode only, there is no overwrite mode. The Ins key, which in word processing normally toggles between these two modes, has another function within Ventura. You should type only one space after full stops. The carriage return key will cause the start of a new paragraph.

49

If you add text within existing text, it will take on the characteristics of the text surrounding it (i.e., font and style). If you start a new paragraph, it will initially be in Body Text style, though it can be tagged to a different style subsequently. If you set a particular font or style while in text mode, text you add will be in this form, unless and until you start a new paragraph, when it will revert to Body Text attributes.

Small text deletions can be performed by placing the cursor and using the backspace (to delete to left) or delete (to delete to right) keys. More extensive deletions (block deletions) can be performed by highlighting the text to be deleted, and pressing the delete (Del) key. To highlight text, you can either place the cursor at the beginning of the text to be deleted, and then drag it to the end, or place the cursor at the beginning, hold down the shift key, and place the cursor at the end.

Blocks of text can also be copied or moved. The difference between these two operations is that copying leaves the text in the original place, as well as a new location, so it appears twice (or more with repeated operations) in the document.

To move text, first highlight it, then select Cut Text from the Edit menu. The text will be removed from the document and stored in memory. Move the cursor to the location where you want to place the text, and click the mouse button. Then select Paste Text from the Edit menu. The Ins key can be used as a keyboard shortcut for this operation. Note that the text remains in memory as well, so it can be pasted two or more times. However, only the most recently cut (or copied) section of text is stored.

It is possible to move text from one file to another by this method, as well as from place to place within one file.

To copy text, first hightlight it, then select Copy Text from the Edit menu. This copies the text to memory, leaving it intact in its original location. The text is copied to a new location (or locations) just as for moving text. In fact, the only difference between these two operations is whether the text is deleted from its original place.

If you copy whole paragraphs with these methods, they will retain their original tags. If you copy parts from the middle of a paragraph into the middle of another paragraph, they will take on the attributes of the surrounding text. However, any parts of the text which have been given special attributes (i.e., italic), and which are copied intact, will retain that attribute. If you make a new paragraph from a middle part of an existing paragraph, it will initially take on Body Text style, regardless of the original style. It can, of course, be tagged to a different style subsequently.

Tags and Effects

Paragraph format tags and character sequences for other features can be inserted into a text file as it is prepared. With a word processor which Ventura supports, it is normally easier to use the WP facilities for the features which Ventura converts (see Chapter 1). However, for other features, and for ASCII files, the following methods must be used.

The sequence for inserting a paragraph tag is:

@Tag Name = Text of paragraph . . .

Here, 'Tag Name' is replaced by the exact name you have given to that paragraph style, matching upper and lower case and including any spaces. Note that there must be a space between the tag name and the ' = ' and the first character of the text. The ' @ ' must be the first character on the first line of the paragraph.

Characters in the Ventura character set which cannot be entered from the keyboard can be used by enclosing the number of the character in angle brackets. For example, the copyright symbol can be inserted as <189> (using the International character set). If you want to insert angle brackets within the text without having them interpreted as part of a character code, you must double them. For example, to include the programming 'not equal to' symbol, ' <> ', you would enter ' <<>> '.

Text attributes, to set fonts and styles (such as bold, italic, etc.) are also entered using angle brackets. Capital letters are used for styles, and can be given singly or in combination. For example, ' <BI> ' would set bold italic. Note that each time you use such an attribute sequence, it resets any attributes already in effect, so if you have set bold with ' <B> ', you need to use ' <BI> ' to set bold italic, and ' <B> ' again will take you back to just bold.

The codes for the various attributes are as follows:

M	Medium weight text
B	Bold
I	Italics
U	Underline
=	Double underline
O	Overscore
X	Strikethrough
S	Small
^	Superscript
v	Subscript

The typeface can be set with ' <Fn> ' when n is replaced with one of the font ID numbers. These will be found in Appendix K of the Ventura reference guide. For example, <F1> will set Courier typeface. <F255> will reset the typeface to the default for the paragraph. Legal font ID numbers are from 1 to 65535.

The point size is set using ' <Pn>', where n is replaced by the point size. For example, <P12> sets 12-point type. As with typefaces, <P255> resets the default for the paragraph.

There are various other attributes which can be set, but they fall beyond the scope of this book. They can all be found in Appendix D of the Ventura reference guide.

One of the best ways of learning how to include these codes within a document is to create a short document, save it as an ASCII file, and import it into Ventura. Then tag paragraphs with various styles, change some of the text to different fonts and styles, and print it. Then load the file back into the word processor or editor, and examine the codes inserted to control the effects.

Chapter 5
GRAPHICS

When a DTP document is to include illustrations, there are several ways in which they can be included. If the finished document is to be printed by a printer, the illustrations can be sent to the printer and included in the document by conventional means, as line or half-tone blocks. Alternatively, the illustrations can be prepared in electronic form, for example by a CAD or paint program, and included in the DTP document. Where illustrations already exist on paper, it is possible for them to be converted into electronic digital form.

Even when illustrations are to be added by the printer, it may be helpful to include them in the DTP document, to indicate position, and to help design the layout on the screen. When this is done, the illustrations should have 'for position only' clearly marked over them.

Adding Graphics
Like text, graphics can often either by drawn within Ventura, or imported from a paint or draw program which has a file format in common. As with text, the latter course is normally the preferable one, as the graphics creation facilities provided are strictly limited.

Ventura can import a wide variety of graphics formats, for both bit-image graphics and vector graphics. The former are normally generated by 'paint' programs, and the latter by 'draw' or CAD programs. Whenever possible, it is best to use a graphics program which is directly supported.

One conversion program is provided with Ventura, on the Utilities disk. It is called DXFTOGEM, and is used to convert files in the AutoCAD/AutoSketch DXF format to the GEM format used by Ventura. This program works well, but cannot convert some features which are not supported by the GEM format (see Chapter 1). It also has some other drawbacks. For example, in the Author's experience, it will not correctly convert filled areas in AutoSketch drawings. Several other CAD/Draw type programs can also save files in DXF format.

Graphics files are loaded in much the same way as text files, by initially selecting Load Text/Picture from the FILES menu, and then filling in the dialogue boxes. You can load more than one file in a single operation, but when doing this all files must be in the same format. If you want to load files of more than one format into a document, this is quite possible, but each type must be loaded in a separate operation.

All graphics are contained in a frame. It is by means of this frame that they can be moved around the screen and (in most cases) scaled and resized. Frames are added by entering frame mode from the Mode selector, and then simply drawing the frame where it is required. If more accurate placing is required than can be done by hand and eye, the frame can be approximately drawn in place, and then adjusted by using the Sizing And Scaling dialogue box from the FRAME menu. Figure 5.1 shows this dialogue box.

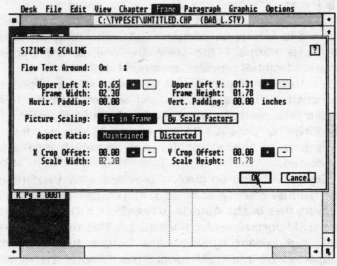

Fig.5.1 The sizing and scaling dialogue

If a frame is active and empty when a graphics file is loaded, the graphic will be placed in that frame. Otherwise, graphics will need to be loaded into frames in the same way as text files, by making a frame active, and then clicking on the name of the file in the file list. A frame can contain only a single graphic, and a graphic cannot flow between two frames in the way a text file can.

By default, when a graphic is placed in a frame, it is adjusted in size to fit in the frame. You can therefore size the graphic simply by adjusting the frame size. If it is important to keep the correct aspect ratio in the graphic (i.e. keep circles circular), you can set Aspect Ratio to Maintained in the Sizing and Scaling dialogue box. The graphic will then be adjusted to fit the frame in one dimension only, the other dimension being adjusted to maintain the ratio.

If you set Picture Scaling to By Scale Factors, you can enter the exact size you want the graphic to be, as Scale Width and Scale Height in the Sizing and Scaling dialogue box. If Aspect Ratio is Maintained, you can set only the width, the height being adjusted as necessary. The X Crop Offset and Y Crop Offset place the graphic within the frame.

The effectiveness of scaling depends on the type of the original graphic. In the case of vector graphics, as produced by drawing or CAD type programs, the scaling can be quite sophisticated. Because of the object-oriented way in which they are stored, they can be scaled up without loss of resolution. In some cases, scaling up can reveal extra detail. However, care may be necessary to ensure that circles remain truly circular.

The main cause of problems with vector graphics is usually any lettering which may be included. In some cases it may be reproduced correctly. In other cases it may appear in quite a different font, or totally the wrong size, or in the wrong place, or both. In general, the best advice is to remove any labels before importing the graphic, and then to relabel it in Ventura using the program's fonts. This will enable the style of lettering to be consistent with the rest of the document, and will probably also give higher quality, as well as avoiding problems with placement. You will need to use a separate frame for each label, and extensive labelling can mean a lot of work.

In the case of bit-image graphics, as produced by drawing type programs, the scaling can only be done in a rather crude way. If a graphic is to be reduced in size by 10 per cent, every tenth row of pixels is simply deleted. A similar increase in size would be obtained by doubling every tenth row. This can disrupt any fill patterns which have been used, and is also a problem with 'dithered' (simulated halftone) scanner graphics. Generally, however, simple line drawings can be scaled without problems, as can scanner graphics scanned in 'line' mode, i.e., without dithering.

There should be no problem with lettering in bit-image graphics, except that it is likely to be of very low quality compared to the DTP fonts, and it will also be distorted by scaling. Again, the best answer is to do any labelling with Ventura after importation, where this is practicable.

Paint Graphics
Paint graphics are produced with programs such as GEM Paint and PC Paintbrush. They are essentially screen-painting programs, and always work at screen resolution, though the drawing you can work on can be bigger than one screen in size. The image you draw is stored as the pixel pattern, not as 'objects'. This allows great flexibility in the drawing, but means that the images cannot be scaled entirely successfully.

If you draw a small circle, and scale it up, it will be the actual drawn pixel pattern which is scaled. This means that steps in the circle will become apparent. (Some people called these 'jaggies'. I don't.) Any fill patterns used can also be distorted and spoiled. However, provided you do not go to extremes, some scaling is certainly possible with acceptable results.

Programs of this sort generally work in colour, or in shades of grey on a monochrome screen. In Ventura, each pixel in a draw-type graphic can be either black or white. It cannot handle colour or grey shades in this type of image. If you import a coloured or shaded image, it will be converted to black and white in a rather arbitrary way, and the results are rarely satisfactory.

Paint graphics are best used for informal illustrations, like cartoons, rather than for more technical or diagrammatic illustrations, for which draw-type programs are more suited. As well as drawing your own graphics of this type, it is possible to buy libraries of 'clip-art' which you can add to your documents, though there may be copyright restrictions on how they may be used.

Drawn Graphics
There are two fairly distinct types of Draw programs. CAD programs like AutoCad and AutoSketch are mainly intended for technical illustration. Line-art programs like GEM Artline and Corel Draw! are intended more for graphic design and special text features. However, the files generated by the two types are treated in the same way by Ventura.

These files store graphics as drawn 'objects'. That is to say, a circle is stored as a circle object, which has a size and position, a line is stored as a line object, and so on. This allows sizing and scaling to be carried out in a much more satisfactory way. No matter how much you scale up a circle, it remains a smooth circle. In fact, as it gets bigger, it gets smoother.

Graphics of this sort can be scaled up and down as much or as little as required. If scaled down too far, however, some features may become too small to reproduce. It is also necessary to take care to scale equally in the vertical and horizontal directions if aspect ratios are to be preserved. Ventura can take care of this automatically by selecting Maintain Aspect Ratio in the Sizing And Scaling dialogue box.

In CAD type programs, there may be two types of font available. The first type, called 'stroke fonts', draws characters as lines in the same way as any other part of the drawing. This type of font normally imports into Ventura without problems. The second type are similar to the fonts used in DTP programs. They give better solidity to lettering, but can cause problems when imported. It is

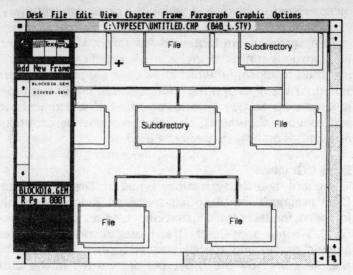

Fig.5.2   An AutoSketch drawing

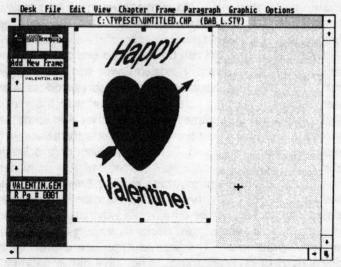

Fig.5.3   An imported GEM Artline graphic

better either to stick to the stroke fonts, or to add lettering after importation. Figure 5.2 shows an AutoSketch
drawing imported into Ventura (via DXFTOGEM) which
uses a stroke font.

Line-art programs like GEM Artline use a system of
'outline' fonts. These allow great flexibility in sizing text,
and special effects, bending and distorting the lettering, are
also possible. GEM Artline is particularly suitable for use
with Ventura, as the versions of GEM used are compatible,
and there are no problems at all importing these graphics.
Figure 5.3 shows a GEM Artline graphic imported into
Ventura, with distorted lettering correctly reproduced.

Colour in drawn graphics is preserved in Ventura, sub-
ject to the limit of eight fixed colours. The colour will be
displayed on a supported colour display, and can also be
printed on a suitable colour printer.

Scanner Graphics

A scanner is the standard method of converting a graphic
in paper form into digital information which can be
included in a DTP document. The paper graphic can be a
line drawing, a photograph, or any artwork of suitable
size which is physically able to be scanned. That last part
mostly means that the artwork should be flat, and, for
some types of scanner, have a stable surface which will not
be disrupted or smudged by the scanning operation. Pastel
and charcoal drawings, for example, are not suitable for
most types of scanner, unless they have been treated with
a fixative.

Photographs for scanning will normally be in the form
of prints. Scanners which can scan transparencies are very
expensive items, though there are bureaux and printing
companies which will scan transparencies for a (considerable) fee. Generally, both colour and black-and-white
prints can be scanned, but the sensing elements in scanners
(charge-coupled devices, or 'CCD's'), whilst panchromatic,
have a considerable bias in their sensitivity towards the
red end of the spectrum. This can mean that flesh tones
in a colour print can reproduce as too light a tone in a
scan, and lips can tend to disappear. To overcome this

problem, some scanners use a light source which is filtered to a yellow-green colour.

Note that, although Ventura can handle 'spot' colour, it cannot handle coloured bit-image graphics, either scanned or drawn. These will be converted into black-and-white on loading, and this conversion rarely works entirely satisfactorily.

Grey Scales and Dithering

When an original having a range of half-tones (that is, shades of grey between black and white), is scanned, some means must be used to represent those grey tones within the file generated by the scanner. There are two ways of doing this.

It is possible to assign a density value to every point scanned. If, for example, each point scanned is given one byte in the file, it can have one of 256 values assigned to it. In fact, only a very few flatbed scanners are capable of generating true grey scale information, and they tend to be the more expensive.

When a file containing true grey-scale information is imported into Ventura, the program can make contrast and density changes to the image, making it possible to fine-tune it for the printer in use.

A disadvantage of the true grey-scale system is that it tends to result in very large files, especially if a large original is scanned at a high resolution. There are, as yet, no true grey-scale printers. This means that when the image is printed, the half-tones have to be produced by varying the spacing of the printer dots. In the dark parts of the picture, most of the possible dots are printed, whereas in the lighter parts fewer are printed. This process is known as dithering.

In order to produce smaller image files, the dithering can be done at an earlier stage, either in the scanner software, or in the scanner itself. When this is done, each point in the scan is either printed or not printed, so can be represented by a single bit in the file. However, when a scan is generated in dithered form, it cannot subsequently be altered either in density or contrast by Ventura.

Dot-pitches, Sizing and Scaling

The dot-pitch of a scanner is the distance between the points on the original at which the scanner takes a reading. It is normally expressed in dots per inch, and may be regarded as a measure of how much detail the scanner can record.

The majority of scanners allow the user to select from a number of dot-pitches. The highest and lowest pitches the Author has come across are 75 and 400 dpi. It may be thought that the higher the dot-pitch the better, but in fact this is not necessarily so. In practice, the lower pitches can be equally, or even more, useful.

Some people have the impression that the scanning pitch must always match the dot-pitch of the printer to be used. This is not correct. Using the dot-pitches allows you some control of the size of the reproduced picture, relative to the size of the original. As each scanned dot will reproduce as one printed dot, if you scan at 300 dpi and use a 300 dpi laser printer, the reproduction will be the same size as the original. If you scan at 150 dpi, however, the reproduction will be half the size of the original. On the other hand, if you scan at 300 dpi and use a 180 dpi dot-matrix printer, the reproduction will be *larger* than the original, in the ratio of 5:3.

The ability to magnify in this way is useful if you have only a hand scanner and want to produce large-size illustrations. By scanning at 400 dpi, if you have a 180 dpi printer you can more than double the size of the original, so that a full A4 page illustration can be produced from an ordinary enprint (4" x 6"). Providing the enprint is reasonably sharp, the quality should be acceptable.

With dithered originals, this is the only method of scaling which should be considered. Most DTP programs do allow scaling of bit-images to fit a frame, but this is done in a relatively crude way. If an image needs to be reduced by 10 per cent in one direction, all that happens is that every tenth row of dots is omitted. If an image is to be scaled up by 10 per cent, every tenth row is doubled. It can be seen that this will have a disastrous result on the carefully designed dither patterns, and will result in all-too-obvious lines and patterns on the picture.

When a scanned image is imported into Ventura, if you select By Scale Factors in Sizing And Scaling, the image will be adjusted to the size of the original. This is fine if your scanner and printer use the same dot pitch. If they do not, you will have to adjust the size to get dot-for-dot reproduction. For example, if you have scanned at 200 dpi and you are using a 180 dpi printer, take the Scale Width as shown in Sizing And Scaling, multiply it by 200 and divide by 180, and enter this as the new scale width. The aspect ratio should be set to Maintained. See Figure 5.4.

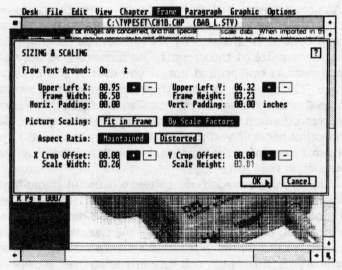

Fig.5.4 Adjusting the size of a scanned image

When viewing scanned images on the screen, remember that these programs always work at printer resolution, and that what you see on the screen is not a pixel-for-dot representation of what will be printed. The screen pixels are much larger than the final printer dots, and this means that the screen quality of dithered images may be quite poor. If you are worried about the final quality, try a test print. Don't judge the quality of an image from what you see on the screen.

It should be understood that you cannot produce more detail in the reproduction by scanning at a finer dot-pitch and then scaling the image down in the DTP program. The limit on the detail which can be shown is set by the printer pitch. The best quality will always be obtained by ensuring that one scan point corresponds exactly to one printer dot.

Scanner Software

When you buy a scanner, of any type, it should be supplied with suitable driver software. As well as providing an interface between the scanner and the computer, this software should allow some control of the scan, and some flexibility of output file format.

The most important thing to check is whether the software for the scanner you intend to buy can generate a file format which Ventura can import. These are the GEM .IMG, PC Paintbrush .PCX, Macintosh Paint .PIC, and .TIF formats. To import Apple Macintosh files requires suitable comms software.

TIFF (same as .TIF) files can contain either bit-image data or true grey-scale information, for those scanners capable of generating it. Ventura uses this format for grey-scale files.

Many scanner control programs can produce output in all of these formats, so that you may have a choice of file type to transfer images from scanner to DTP program. As far as the quality of the image is concerned, it probably won't make a blind bit of difference which you use. However, Ventura can handle .IMG files easier than other types, but the .TIF format must be used for true grey-scale images.

The area which you scan will not always be the exact area you wish to use. A good scanner program will allow you to 'cut out' the part of the scanned image you wish to use, and save only that part of the image to disk. This feature is vital with Ventura, as it does not include facilities for cropping images after importation.

Orientation is another problem. If you want to scan a full A4 illustration, it can only be placed in the scanner one way round, but you may want it to appear in your document vertically up a page (portrait orientation), or horizontally across a page (landscape orientation). The scanner program should allow you to rotate the image before saving it to disk. You may be able to rotate the image by 90 degrees in one direction only, so care may be necessary to ensure you place the original in the scanner correctly, otherwise the rotated version could be upside down! Other programs allow rotation to any orientation, in steps of 90 degrees.

Ventura Graphics
Ventura includes limited facilities for adding graphics directly. These are limited to drawing lines, circles (and ellipses), and boxes with square or rounded corners. The circles and boxes can be solid, hollow, or filled with a shade, colour or fill pattern. There is also a facility for box text, which enables you to draw a box and put text in it.

These facilities are not really intended for adding illustrations to documents. They are much more for adding decorative features to documents, such as rules between headings and text (as distinct from underlining). Directly-drawn graphics do not have to be in frames. This makes for easy placement anywhere on the page. Each drawn element has instead a set of 'handles' by which it may be resized. These are the small squares around the circle in Figure 5.5.

To aid accurate placement, an invisible 'grid' can be drawn on the page, and graphics elements can be made to 'snap' to this grid. The size of the grid can be set by the user, and snap can be turned on or off as required. See Figure 5.6.

Figure 5.7 shows the Fill Attributes dialogue box. This is used for filled shapes. Only shapes drawn with the circle and box tools can be filled. A shape made up of separate lines cannot be filled. Line thickness can also be selected, both for lines and the outlines of shapes. Ends of lines can

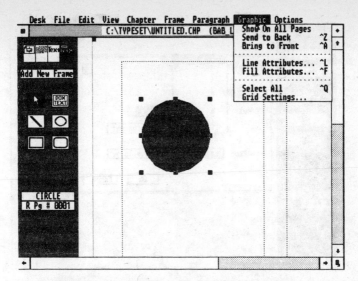

Fig.5.5   The 'handles' around a graphics element

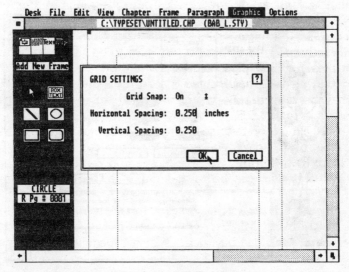

Fig.5.6   The grid settings dialogue box

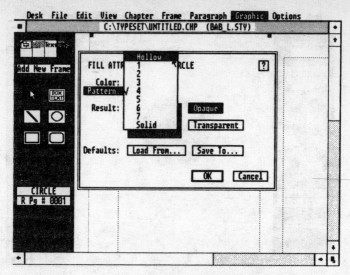

Fig.5.7 Setting fill attributes

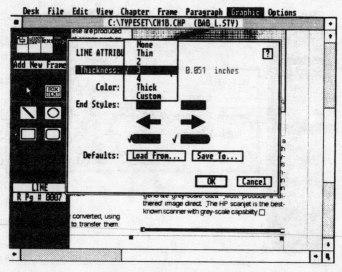

Fig.5.8 Setting line attributes

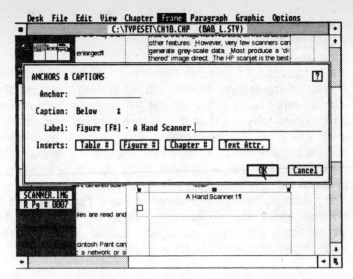

Fig.5.9   Captioning an illustration

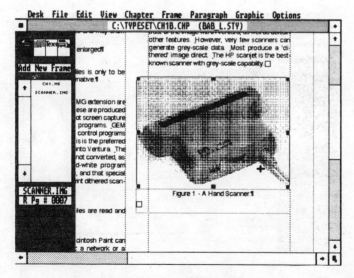

Fig.5.10   A captioned graphic

69

be square, round, or arrowhead. Figure 5.8 show the dialogue box.

Captions

Any graphic in a frame can have a caption attached to that frame. If the graphic is then moved around the page, the caption will always move with it. Figures can be numbered automatically, so that if you insert a new graphic into a chapter, all figures coming after it will have their numbers automatically adjusted. Figure 5.9 shows the dialogue box to add a caption, and Figure 5.10 shows the result of this.

By default, the caption uses the Body Text font, and is centred under the illustration. However, these can be altered from Paragraph mode, and individual parts of the caption can be changed in style from Text mode.

Chapter 6

PUTTING IT ALL TOGETHER

The steps in preparing a document, in the order in which you would normally carry them out, are:

1. Design or load a style sheet.
2. Import the main text file and place it.
3. Go through the text file, tagging paragraphs, etc.
4. Add any incidental text, and any illustrations.

This order is not sacrosanct, but it is the order which will generally involve the least work, and in particular the least repeated effort, with changes undoing earlier work. The earlier chapters described the techniques involved. This chapter shows how to use them to design a document.

Adding Frames and Pages
When putting a document together, it will nearly always be necessary to add some frames to it. Additional pages may also be necessary if you want to use full-page illustrations or substantial inserted text.

A new frame can simply be added anywhere you want it by simply clicking on Add New Frame in Frame mode, and drawing it where required. It can also be sized and placed to within 1/100 of an inch, using the Sizing And Scaling dialogue. All added frames are initially repelling by default, so if the frame is placed over existing text, the text will flow around it. All text below the frame will be moved down, and if it is in the page frame, extra pages will be added automatically at the end of the document to take any overflow.

If text in a frame other than the page frame is displaced, it is up to you to make sure it is not lost. You may need to enlarge the frame containing it, or provide another frame for it to wrap into.

If you import a text file into an added frame, only as much text as will fit into the frame will be placed. You have to add further frames and manually place the remainder of the text. Once this is done, if any of the text is displaced, by adding illustrations, for instance, the text will flow between the frames, but any overflow from the last will be unplaced. You need to check for this.

To remove a text file or illustration from a frame, you must be in frame mode. You then select the frame, and then select Remove Text/File in the EDIT menu. You can then choose to remove the file from List Of Files, which removes it from the chapter entirely, or from Frame, which removes it from the frame, but leaves it on the assignment list, so that it can be placed elsewhere.

Extra pages can be added anywhere in the document, including before the first page and after the last, by choosing Insert/Remove Page from the PAGE menu. You can choose to insert the page before or after the current page. This new page will have a page frame with the style sheet characteristics. The original text file will flow around this page. You can put any text or illustrations you like onto this new page.

Note that if you import a substantial text file into the page frame on an inserted page, it will work just like importing a text file into a chapter. If the file is too big for the page, extra pages will be added automatically, after the inserted page and before the rest of the original text file.

Inserted pages can be removed by using the same menu option, but before this is done, all text files must be removed from the page(s).

Mixing Text and Graphics
Normally, text and graphics will be mixed on the same page, though there may well be pages which are text only, or which have a full-page graphic. The system of frames is used to allow text and graphics to be mixed in an attractive way, but avoiding unintentional overlaps.

The normal way of preventing text from being hidden is to make the graphics frames 'repel' text. In this way, if a graphics frame is placed over text frames or columns, the position of the text will be adjusted so that it 'flows'

Desk File Edit View Chapter Frame Paragraph Graphic Options
C:\TYPESET\CH1B.CHP (BAB_L.STY)
Add New Frame
CH1.MS
SCANNER.IMG
EMPTY
R Pg # 0003

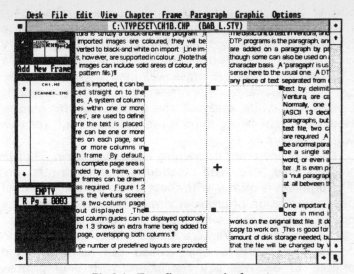

Fig.6.1 Text flow around a frame

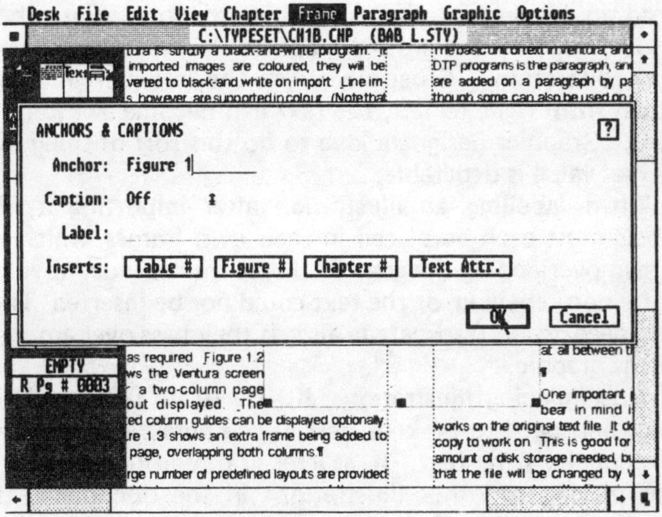

Desk File Edit View Chapter Frame Paragraph Graphic Options
C:\TYPESET\CH1B.CHP (BAB_L.STY)
ANCHORS & CAPTIONS
Anchor: Figure 1
Caption: Off
Label:
Inserts: Table # Figure # Chapter # Text Attr.
OK Cancel
EMPTY
R Pg # 0003

Fig.6.2 Setting an Anchor Name

around the frame (see Figure 6.1). It is also possible for frames to be set so that they do not repel text. This can be used to allow text and graphics to be deliberately superimposed, but the background 'tint' of the frame must also be considered. Frames will have an opaque background by default. This means that any text passing behind the white areas of the graphic will be hidden. However, if the background is set to transparent, the text will 'show through'.

There is one point of warning to be given here. Though Ventura may have these capabilities, not all printers do. The problem is mostly with those which use some form of page compilation or page description language. These may not be able to cope with superimposition, or may place restrictions on it. Ventura comes with a demonstration document, CAPABILI.CHP, which can be loaded and printed to discover any restrictions with your printer.

It is possible to flow text around a complex shape by making the main frame containing the graphic non-repelling, and then drawing a series of overlapping, empty, but repelling frames over the graphic to clear the text from behind it. This can, however, be a lot of work, and you need to be sure of the capabilities of your printer here also. Irregular text around graphics also needs to be used with discretion. Especially when the left margin slopes down from right to left, the text can become awkward to read. Graphics designers love to do this sort of thing, but its real value is debatable.

When labelling an illustration after importing it, the labels must each be placed in their own frames, which are drawn overlapping the graphic. These frames must obviously be non-repelling, or the text could not be inserted. They will need to be transparent also, if they pass over any part of the graphic.

When placing illustrations, if they relate to part of the text, and need to be kept near it, it is possible to insert an 'anchor' into the text. If, as a result of editing changes, or the placing of other illustrations in the document, the illustration and anchor become displaced, you can select Re-Anchor Frames in the CHAPTER menu to move the frame back to the anchor.

This is a multi-step procedure. Firstly, you must select the frame you want to anchor. Note that it is the frame, not the file it contains, which is anchored. Then, you choose Anchors And Captions from the FRAME menu, and enter a name for your anchor (see Figure 6.2).

The anchor must now be inserted into the text. This is done from text mode. The cursor must be placed at the point in the text where you want to anchor the frame. Then choose Insert Special Item from the EDIT menu. A selection box will appear, from which you must choose Frame Anchor. Enter the name of your anchor into the dialogue box which appears next (Figure 6.3).

You can then choose where you want your frame to be placed, relative to the anchor. The options are to have the frame on the same page as the anchor, above the anchor line, below the anchor line, or at the anchor position. The last allows a small anchor to be inserted into the text line. The anchor appears in the text as a degree symbol. This is not, of course, printed.

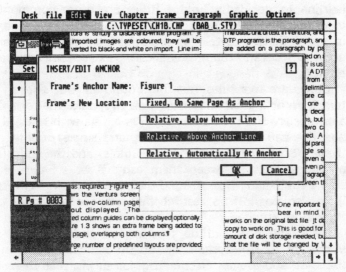

Fig.6.3 Placing a frame anchor in text

When you subsequently choose Re-Anchor Frames from the CHAPTER menu, you can choose to re-anchor frames for the current page only, or for all pages. Note that re-anchoring a page at a time could cause further separations elsewhere, unless you work from the beginning of the chapter to the end.

Decorative Features

Apart from actual graphics, Ventura can produce decorative features on the page. These include rules, boxes, tints, and others.

Rules are simply straight lines drawn on the page. Rules are commonly used to separate text columns, and indeed Ventura puts a rule between columns by default, or to separate sections of text. They can also be used to underline headings (though this can appear fussy if overdone), and to separate the top of pages, containing the headings, from the body of the page, containing the text. When this is done, it is often advisable, to maintain balance, to rule off the bottom of the page as well.

Rules are produced with the graphics line-drawing facility, and can be drawn in different widths, from a hairline to decidedly bold. Rules are more commonly used in things like newspapers and journals, where text is fairly densely set, than in books, where it is more usual to separate columns by allowing extra space between them.

Boxes are like rules, but run around all four sides of a text item or a graphic. In Ventura they take the form of a border around the containing frame. As with rules, the box line can be of user-set width, and single, double, or triple. Both the width(s) of the line(s) and the width(s) of the space(s) between them can be set. Figure 6.4 shows the Ruling Box Around dialogue box. In Ventura, it is also possible to restrict the 'box' to one, two or three sides only.

Since the box will be the size of the frame, it is important to adjust the frame to the size which will give the best appearance on the page, ensuring that there is not too much surplus space in the frame below the text,

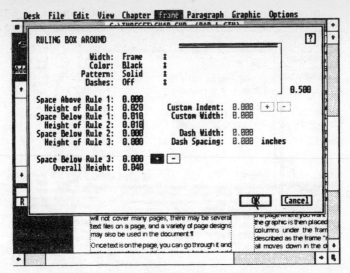

Fig.6.4   The Ruling Box Around dialogue box

for example. An exception to this would be if you were boxing all the body text columns in a publication, and you wanted the boxes on all the pages to be the same size.

Boxes are most often used to highlight paragraphs of particular importance or interest. They can also be used to enclose headings. A 'box out' is a common technique in magazine publishing. Here, a quotation, normally an eye-catching one, taken from the text of the article, is placed in a box and usually printed in a larger type size than the body text.

Tints are a pattern of fine dots which form a background to a frame. Like boxing, this makes the frame stand out from the rest of the text, and it can be used for the same purposes as, or in conjunction with, boxing. The tint is normally controllable in stages, expressed in percentages, from very light to black.

Care must be used with tints around the middle of the range, as they can make the text difficult to read, unless a large font size is employed. With dark tints, of course, the text will normally be printed in white. Before using

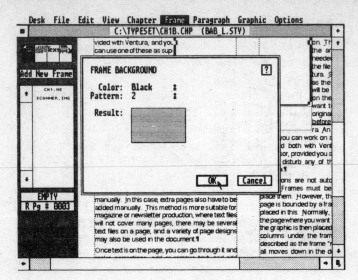

Fig.6.5   Setting a background tint

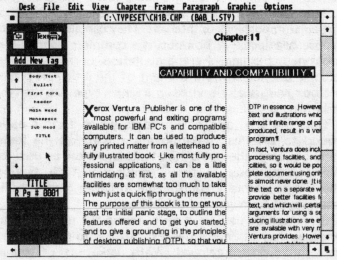

Fig.6.6   A paragraph with a drop cap

78

white on dark text, you should test your printer's capabilities, as it is not possible to print this on all types. Tint effects may not be very pleasant on low-resolution (dot matrix) printers. Figure 6.5 shows the background tint dialogue box.

It is common practice to in some way enhance the first paragraph of a feature. There are several ways in which this is done. The first word, or line, of the paragraph may be printed in a larger and/or emboldened form of the body text font, or the whole paragraph may be printed in a larger size, or with extra leading. All of these can be done with standard facilities. However, the most popular way is to print the first letter of the paragraph in a very large size, perhaps matching the headline font. Ventura has a built-in feature to do this, and the vertical placing of the 'big cap' is adjustable. If it is adjusted so that the top is aligned with the tops of the rest of the first line, it is called a 'drop cap'. This is the most popular style. Figure 6.6 shows a paragraph with a drop-cap.

More than one of these first-paragraph features may be combined. For instance, you might combine a drop cap with printing the whole paragraph in a larger size than the body text. As with so many other aspects of design, one must be careful not to overdo it, however.

Bullets are a device which are often used at the beginning of paragraph. They are particularly used for a series of paragraphs which form a list of features. The 'Bullet' is a special character, such as a large dot, an arrow, a star (distinct from the normal asterisk), or a hand. There are many others. When a bullet paragraph style is used in Ventura, the remainder of the paragraph is indented automatically in line with the first text character after the bullet (see Figure 6.7).

Bullets and large capitals are set from the Special Effects dialogue box. This is shown in Figure 6.8.

Design Principles
Of course, the placing of text and graphics is more than just getting all the material into the document. The way in which a document is laid out can greatly contribute to,

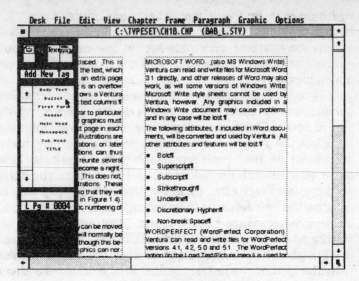

Fig.6.7   Bullet paragraphs

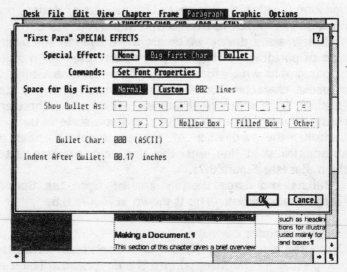

Fig.6.8   The Special Effects dialogue box

or detract from, the effectiveness of the document.

One of the most important things is to be consistent throughout the document. Using the same style sheet throughout the document, with the same typefaces and sizes throughout for the same purposes (body text, sub-headings, headings, captions), helps here. It is also important to use the same approach for inserting illustrations, either aligning them with the text columns, or placing them across columns and flowing the text around them, or keeping text and illustrations in separate areas.

You must always consider whether the paper will be printed on both sides, or on one side only. In one-sided printing, the blank pages opposite can be ignored, but in two-sided printing, the two facing pages must be considered as a single entity for design purposes. They need to be designed either to provide a symmetrical layout around the central gutter, or to have a harmonious asymmetrical design.

Whether single or double sided, you also need to consider the type of binding to be used for the final document. If ring-binding is to be used, sufficient space must be allowed for the punch holes. With plastic channel binders you also need to allow extra space on the inner edges. If a document is to be printed and bound professionally, you should seek the printer's advice on how much binding width to allow.

One of the most important considerations in any document is readability, and perhaps the most important factor here is the width of the text columns. They should generally be made about 65 characters. If you make columns narrower than this, the text will read jerkily, and there will also be an excessive amount of hyphenation. If wider, readers will tend to 'lose their place' as they go from the end of one line to the beginning of the next. If it is essential to use a column width greater than 65 characters, this problem can usually be reduced by increasing the leading, or space between lines, but of course this reduces the amount of text which can be placed on a page.

It is also important to remember that if you insert too many illustrations with text flowed around them, you are in effect narrowing the column width over a major part of the document. If a document contains a lot of illustrations, it is usually preferable to avoid this type of layout. The width of illustrations should be adjusted to the width of a column, or multiple columns, or text and illustrations should be separated vertically (e.g. text at the top of a page, illustration below). Alternatively, text and illustrations can be placed on separate pages.

The spacing between text columns, known as the 'gutters', is also important. If too narrow, the eye may tend to try to cross to the next column instead of moving down and across to the start of the next line. Normally, narrower gutters can be used if the text columns are justified on both margins rather than if the right margin is left ragged. Wide gutters can give an attractive, clean-looking page layout, but do of course, reduce the amount of text to a page.

The gutters are a part of what is called the 'white space' on a page. This is simply blank areas between the text and graphics items. If very little white space is left, the document will appear crowded, fussy, and difficult to read. I expect we have all seen club newsletters with the typewriter margins set right out to the sides of the paper and the line spacing set to minimum. This is the ideal way to get the maximum number of words on a page and also to ensure that the minimum of them are read.

If it really is necessary to cram text onto the page, with narrow line spacing, readability can be maintained by keeping the columns and gutters narrow, and making extensive use of fine vertical and horizontal rules to separate them. This is the typical style of newspapers.

Magazines normally use more white space, and generally the more up-market the magazine, the more white space. One should beware of going too far, however. If there is more space than text, the effect is to imply that the text is not very important, and any illustrations become paramount. In fashion magazines, this may be quite deliberate, of course.

When setting the dimensions for gutters, etc., you need to be consistent in the vertical and horizontal directions to maintain a balanced appearance. If you increase the space between columns, you also need to increase the vertical space between paragraphs, and perhaps the leading too. You also need to allow more space around any illustrations let into the text.

Chapter 7

ADDING FONTS

A font is a collection of characters in a particular size, style and typeface. If you change any of these, you have a different font. Selection of fonts, more than any other factor, will influence the appearance and effectiveness of your finished documents.

To take the factors which define a font one by one, the collection of characters is termed the 'character set'. Ventura can use the Ventura International Character set or the Ventura U.S. Character Set, which has fewer characters in it. It also uses special 'Symbol' and 'Dingbat' character sets for these special fonts.

The size of a font is given in 'points'. Each point is approximately equal to 1/72 of an inch. A 12-point character is therefore 1/6 of an inch high. This size refers to the height of a normal capital letter. However, it is normal for the sizes of fonts as given for DTP purposes to include the inter-line spacing, or 'leading' (pronounced like the metal), so the actual height of the characters will normally be less than the nominal point size.

The range of point sizes you can use will be set primarily by the DTP program, and secondarily by the printer, as will the increments in which you can specify sizes. For Ventura, the smallest size you can use is 6-point. For display fonts, the largest size Ventura will load is 36-point. For HP LaserJet and compatible printers, the largest size is the same. For 24-pin dot-matrix printers it is 60-point, and for most other dot-matrix printers 99-point.

The style of a font means whether the letters are normal (called roman), italic, bold, or bold italic. Though you can have separate fonts for each style, it is not always necessary to do so. Ventura can generate an italic or bold style from the normal roman typeface, though this will not be quite the same as the 'real thing'. Not all typefaces will be found in all styles. Zapf Chancery, for instance, only normally comes in normal-weight italic.

Devices and Font Types

It is necessary to specify the device for which a font is designed, be it a printer or a screen. Printer fonts will differ depending on the resolution which the printer can produce, and where the fonts are to be stored before use, either in the computer only, in the printer only, or at some stage transferred from computer to printer. The situation with screen fonts is simpler, as they only ever need to be stored in the computer.

With dot-matrix and inkjet printers, and some laser printers, each page of output is produced in memory (this may include 'slave files' on disk) and then sent to the printer as a 'graphics dump', meaning that the computer directly controls each pin, nozzle or laser pulse during the printing operation. In this case, the fonts are always stored in the computer, and will be in a file form suitable for Ventura. Fonts of this type are termed 'bit-maps', because each file contains maps or patterns of the dots which go to make up each character. This type of font allows the greatest flexibility (except as regards size), as during page generation Ventura can, if required, manipulate the bit-maps to alter the character style.

With some laser printers, the font files are stored in the computer in a form essentially similar to bit-maps, that is, as patterns of dots, but instead of each page being generated in the computer, the fonts to be used are downloaded at the start of printing into memory within the printer. The page is then created within the printer from instructions sent from the computer. The Hewlett-Packard LaserJet printers using the H-P Page Compilation Language (PCL) are the best-known examples of this. This method of printing is inherently less flexible than page production in the computer, but may be quicker as the fonts only need to be down-loaded once for each printing session. Fonts of this type are called 'soft fonts'.

The third possible variant is the use of a Page Compilation Language, of which Adobe PostScript is the best known, and the industry standard. It is used by some laser printers (for example the Apple LaserWriters), and also by professional phototypesetters, such as those made by Linotronic. In PostScript printers, the fonts are stored in the printer as outlines, the shape of each character described as lines and curves independent of dimension. These outlines are scaled to any required size and filled in as required. These 'outline fonts' are stored in the printer or phototypesetter, though it is also possible to down-load additional outlines to most PostScript printers, depending on the amount of memory available within the printer.

Screen fonts are an entirely separate thing to the printer fonts. If you want your printer fonts to be displayed correctly on screen, you will need matching screen fonts. If you do not have an exact match, Ventura will normally use Swiss or Dutch (supplied as standard) in the nearest available size.

Ventura will display a document in (approximately) actual size, in double size to allow detail work, and half-size, to allow a full page (or two facing pages) to be displayed on-screen. To accommodate all these variations, you may need to have screen fonts in double and half the sizes of your printer fonts. You can keep the number of screen fonts you need within bounds by choosing a suitable progression of printer font sizes.

Adding Fonts
Ventura is supplied with two typefaces, Swiss and Dutch, plus a symbol typeface, in a range of point sizes. Exactly what sizes you get varies, depending on what printer you are using. You may also get additional typefaces, such as Courier.

Fonts can be purchased in 'ready to run' form, where you buy a particular typeface in a particular size, but it is now much more normal to buy a font generator program, which uses outline fonts, the same in principle as those used in PostScript devices, and generates bit-map or soft fonts in any required size (within program and hardware limits) for any supported screen and/or printer.

The two best-known suppliers of font generators are Bitstream Fontware of Cambridge, Massachusetts, and GST, who supply the Typografica font generators and who, by coincidence, come from Cambridge, England. These font generators are similar in principle but there are differences in practice.

Bitstream Fontware kits are normally supplied to work with one application only. Ventura is supplied with the appropriate kit, and with outline fonts for Swiss, Dutch, Courier and possibly others. Other outlines may be purchased, but are quite expensive.

The Typografica font generator, on the other hand, can be used with a wide variety of applications, as well as screens and printers. When you buy a Typografica outline font, the generator program comes with it. You can also buy collections of fonts, at a cost saving compared with buying them individually. The GST product is considerably less expensive than the Bitstream.

The fonts from the two kits are a match for overall quality, but there are differences between them. In particular, the normal-weight Typografica fonts are a little lighter than the Bitstream equivalents. Which you prefer is really a matter of taste, but it does mean that it is not a good idea to mix fonts from the two sources on the same typeface.

Though there are detail differences between them, using the two kits is similar in principle. It is important, firstly, to ensure the kit is correctly installed according to the instructions. The Bitstream kit in particular uses several subdirectories, and it is important that the various files used are placed correctly. Also, some files may be supplied on the distribution disks in a compressed form, and need to be decompressed as part of installation. It is not sufficient to simply copy all the files onto a hard disk. Though the Typografica kit can be used on a machine with two floppy disk drives, as DTP is not really practical without a hard disk, it will be assumed here that a hard disk is in use. The Bitstream kits can only be used on a hard disk.

Once the kit is installed, and the font outlines added, font generation can begin. In the case of the Typografica kit, you must specify the application for which you wish to generate fonts. With both kits, you must specify which printer and screen you will be using, from those supported. If the actual printer you will be using is not listed, you may be able to select a compatible printer. For example, many 24-pin dot-matrix printers will use the same fonts as the Epson LQ series, as will the HP PaintJet in graphics mode (i.e., not down-loading the fonts as 'soft fonts', which are different). LaserJet fonts can be used with the HP DeskJet Printer.

The next step is to select the typefaces in which you want to generate the fonts. With Typografica you can only generate fonts in one typeface at a time. With Bitstream, you can generate fonts in several typefaces in one session. For each typeface, you may have a choice of up to four styles, depending on what outlines are available, and have been installed. You specify which point sizes you wish to generate for each style in each typeface.

All the fonts you wish to generate must use the same character set. If you try to use an inappropriate character set, generation will be halted with error messages, as the kit will not be able to find appropriate outlines for some of the characters. Most straightforward alphanumeric fonts will use the same character set. This problem will normally only arise if you are generating symbol or Dingbat fonts. These need to be generated separately to alphanumeric fonts, and to each other.

In the case of the Typografica kit, you can choose to generate screen fonts or printer fonts only, or both in the same range of point sizes. The Bitstream kit lets you specify screen and printer sizes separately. If you want to make extra screen sizes for the half and double size screen displays with the Typografica kit, these must be made in a separate operation. In such cases, you may prefer to keep screen font and printer font generation separate.

Font generation takes a considerable time, especially if you are generating large sizes, or producing a lot of fonts in one go. When you have specified all the sizes you wish to make, the kits will give you an estimate of how long the operation will take. In the Author's experience, these estimates are reasonably accurate, the Bitstream kit being perhaps a bit optimistic. An advantage of the Bitstream kit is that it also tells you if you have sufficient disk space to take the finished fonts.

The generator kits will normally place the fonts directly into the appropriate subdirectories. The kits are normally set up to use the default directories, for example the \VENTURA directory. If you have your applications installed in a non-standard way, or you want to direct the font files elsewhere (perhaps onto floppy disks), you may need to alter the kit setup.

When producing full sets of fonts, the time taken can easily be half an hour to an hour, so this is a job where you need to set the computer going, and then go away and do something else until it has finished. The generator programs are quite robust and not inclined to crash, so this is quite safe. The Bitstream kit does have a stop in it, but this usually occurs, if it is going to, at the time-estimate stage, where it sometimes crashes with a 'Division by zero' error. The cause seems to be trying to generate too many fonts in one go.

You do need to be sure the kit is actually generating the fonts before leaving it. Problems can arise if you are directing the finished fonts to floppy disk. Even if you have a hard disk, you may want to store most of your fonts on floppies, and just load the ones for current use onto your hard disk, in which case it can be a good idea to generate them directly onto the floppies. If you do this, the kit is likely to give a message to insert the disk and 'Press any key' at some stage. Obviously you must get past this stage before leaving the computer to get on with it.

The kit may want to put screen and printer fonts on separate screen and printer disks, depending on which application the fonts are for. In such a case, you may need to be in attendance to change disks when required. Again, it may be better here to make screen and printer font generation completely separate operations.

Width Files

Ventura uses width (.WID) files to tell it the height and width of each character. These files also tell the program what fonts it has available. You can have several width files, but only one can be loaded at a time. Each .STY file has a width file associated with it.

The Bitstream kit generates a width file direct. It may be possible to use this directly. However, it is normally recommended that this file be merged with an existing Ventura width file. This will ensure that the format is correct.

Typografica makes a separate width file for each font. These must be turned into a .WID file using the utility VFMTOWID.EXE which is supplied on the Ventura utilities disk. To use this, it must be copied into the sub-directory containing the new fonts. Typografica also generates a list file (normally called TYPOGRAF.LST), listing the separate width files, and to use VFMTOWID, you simply make the subdirectory containing it current (using the DOS CHDIR command if necessary) and enter at the DOS prompt:

VFMTOWID TYPOGRAF.LST

This generates the width file. Again, it may be possible to use this direct, but it is recommended to merge it with an existing Ventura width file. This is done from within Ventura.

Merging Width Files

To merge width files, you first select Set Printer Info from the OPTIONS menu. If the width table with which you want to merge is that shown in the Set Printer Info dialogue box (see Figure 7.1), click on OK. Otherwise, click on Load Different Width Table. In this case, you will be presented with a selector box from which you can choose.

Next choose Add/Remove Fonts from the OPTIONS menu. It is a good idea at this stage to choose Save As New Width Table (see Figure 7.2). By doing this, you leave the original table unmodified. Next choose Merge Width Tables, and select the table you want to merge from the selector box. Click on OK, and the tables will be merged. You can now use your new fonts.

91

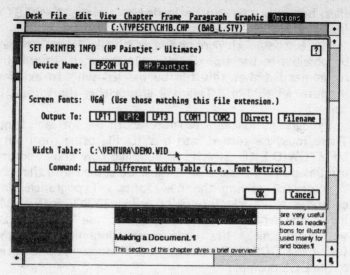

Fig.7.1   The Set Printer Info dialogue box

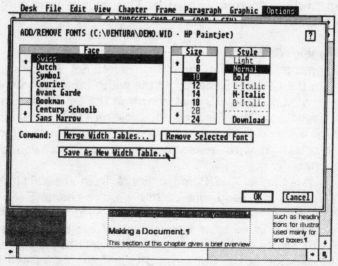

Fig.7.2   The Add/Remove Fonts dialogue box

Normally, you should be careful to ensure that your old and new width tables are for the same printer. However, it is possible to merge tables for different printers, provided the fonts are truly compatible. This may be necessary if the actual printer you are using is one supported by Ventura, but not by the font generator kit.

Index

Notes

Notes

Notes

Notes

Notes